Department of Education and Science

HISTORY IN THE PRIMARY AND SECONDARY YEARS

An HMI View

London
Her Majesty's Stationery Office

CONTENTS

ACKNOWLEDGEMENTS

1 **Queen Christina of Sweden**   The Mansell Collection

2 **Lindow Man – "Pete Marsh"**   Reproduction by courtesy of the Trustees of the British Museum

3 **War time evacuees**   The Mansell Collection

4 **Child dressed as knight**   David Sylvester HMI

5 **Medieval knights**   The Mansell Collection

6 **'Your Country Needs You' – Kitchener recruiting poster**   Imperial War Museum

7 **US recruiting poster**   Imperial War Museum

8 **German Poster**   Imperial War Museum

9 **The coming of the National Grid**   General Electric Review

10 **A Macclesfield classroom at the turn of the century**   From the Macclesfield Silk Heritage Collection

11 **1980s children re-enacting a Victorian schoolroom scene**   Daily Telegraph

12 **"Howe you ought to hold your penne"**   Bodleian Library

13 **Nat Love**   SREB Western American Library

14 **Spanish Republican cartoon**   Reproduced by courtesy of the Trustees of the British Museum

15 **Surgery 1970**   SREB St James' Hospital, Leeds

16 **Mary Seacole**

17 **Buddha**   Reproduced by courtesy of the Trustees of the British Museum

18 **Black servicemen in World War II**   West Indian Servicemen Association

19 **Children using computers**   Microelectronics Education Programme

20a **Early nineteenth century map**

20b **Aerial view of Tower Hamlets**   Tower Hamlets Local History Library

21 **"Question Time" BBC television**   BBC Copyright

22 **"East meets West" – Whitechapel High Street, 1981**   P.D. Barkshire

23 **Lewis Chessman**   Reproduced by courtesy of the Trustees of the British Museum

24 **Christ and dividers**   National Library of Vienna

1 INTRODUCTION

Historians are dangerous people. They are capable of upsetting everything. NIKITA KHRUSHCHEV.

History matters because it is concerned with evidence about human beings who have actually lived and with how human lives have changed through time. It is concerned with explanations and origins and with the contemporary world as much as with the distant past. It demands evidence to support statements about human beings, and it depends on skills of reasoning, criticism and communication. History is concerned not with the conveying of accepted facts but with the making of informed judgements, and to the displaying of the evidence on which those judgements are made.

The concerns of history are neither narrow nor insular. Without an historical perspective, we lack a crucial way of looking at and understanding human society. Thinking about the past must be part of our concern for the present and the future. In this way, history contributes to the personal development of ourselves and our pupils, and to the general education of us all. But it is not just an activity for the classroom, the library or the examination hall. From it springs a range of individual interests, hobbies, and enthusiasms. The evidence for this is clear. Visits to country houses, castles and museums, the sales of paperback books, the popularity of television series about the past, and war games, all remind us that history is a vital part of our leisure interests. Without a sense of history, not only would the curricula of our schools be the poorer, but so too would our personal lives and our ability to relate them to a bewildering contemporary world.

History in the primary and secondary years aims to stimulate discussion. It is therefore not prescriptive. However, its assumptions are based on the belief that teachers of history are under an obligation to define the nature and particular preoccupations of history and its contribution to the whole school curriculum. Most children between the ages of 5 and 14 spend time studying it, as do about half of pupils over the age of 14. History teachers need to say why this should continue to be so and why public resources should be spent on it.

This publication is concerned with the age range 5 to 16. These are the years of compulsory schooling during which all children will be educated in at least two, and many in three, schools. Although the system imposes such breaks, there should be a continuity in children's experience and learning that is recognised and supported if the investment in education – and in history teaching specifically – is to field a high return to individuals and society.

Children's learning, despite changes of school, should present some coherence so that the demands made at the end, say, of one year or four years of learning should be more difficult and challenging than those made at the beginning. Too often the difference measured between young people studying history at the age of 16 and those studying it at the age of 9 or 10 is solely in terms of an increase in information, and this is a tradition that dies hard. Such a limited and modest objective threatens the enthusiasm and love of the past that many young children possess and places an undue emphasis on factual recall, often equating hard, boring routine work with high standards. But if other objectives are to be achieved, means of assessment have to be devised so that teachers can be informed of their pupils' progress. Effective and varied methods of assessment not only help to identify and encourage the acquisition of historical and study skills, they can also profoundly affect teaching methods.

History in the primary and secondary years is written for history teachers, but it may be of interest to parents and pupils, to the governors of schools, to local education authorities, and to education committees. It complements *History from 5 to 16* to be published shortly after the appearance of this document in the Curriculum Matters discussion series – designed to seek views and stimulate debate on the curriculum. *History in the primary and secondary years* not only contributes to the debate but also offers some guidelines for improving practice.

Oh no! Not in Castleford! Maybe if I lived down South. (A schoolboy, being asked if the events in which he might be involved could ever be recorded for the future.)

DENIS SHEMILT

Many children seem to have an innate curiosity about the past. Their comics and games, literature, songs and rhymes suggest that it is a natural part of their culture. The lives and deeds of individual heroes and heroines often immediately catch hold of their imagination and seize their attention.

But history also prepares young people for the world they live in and for their adult life. All pupils live in a socially complex and culturally varied society and in an interdependent world of instant communication. They live in a rapidly changing, and sometimes threatening, environment. They are constantly confronted by persuasion from political parties, pressure groups, the media and advertisers. At 16 some will be members of a trades union; at 18 all will have the vote. Young people will be helped to cope with a bewildering world if they have some understanding of political and economic history, demonstrating the use and abuse of political power, the long-term effects of policies, and the complexity of cause and effect. But their effectiveness as citizens will depend above all on the crucial historical skill of assessing and evaluating the record of human behaviour. Without an understanding of history, young people will enter the worlds of work, citizenship and leisure

blinkered and partly uncomprehending. The initial interest of young children in the past is haphazard and unschooled. History teaching enables children to identify and acquire certain skills and perspectives that support and develop their interest in and knowledge of the past. Its principle characteristics should be the development of:

An awareness of the nature of evidence

So the first lesson that historians are entitled to teach is the austere one: not to generalise from false premises based on inadequate evidence. PROFESSOR MICHAEL HOWARD

All historical judgements depend on the evidence available. The range of that evidence may be very diverse: documents, artefacts, buildings, maps, diagrams and statistics, pictures (including those on television and in the cinema), and the memories of people still alive. Even the youngest pupil can be aware of this diversity. Historical evidence may be difficult to interpret and is always incomplete. As pupils grow older, their knowledge and skills, and their growing experience and emotional maturity, will enable them to interpret and evaluate it more effectively. Because of the range and diversity of the evidence, and the possible interpretations of it, historical judgements are always provisional and tentative. Thus a study of the past can begin to encourage a measure of informed doubt ('We cannot be sure'),

CRISTINA REGINA SVECIÆ, ETC,
1 Queen Christina of Sweden

or responsible scepticism ('How do we know this to be true?'), and an acceptance that statements about people depend on rational thought based on evidence. There is no reason why an awareness of evidence should not permeate the teaching of history for all pupils, however young.

A 9 year old boy had painted a picture of an early nineteenth century child factory worker. 'How do you know he looked like that?', he was asked. The pupil was able to point to a photocopy of the Factory Commissioners' Report made on a visit to the part of the West

Midlands where the school now is. Each witness was described in the Report. The boy's painting was his interpretation of the evidence.

A mixed ability class of 12 year olds in a comprehensive school were looking at pictures of the 'Bayeux Tapestry. 'How do you know that these pictures are telling the truth?', they were asked. 'It all depends who made it', replied one boy. 'It is the same as war films, isn't it?', added another. The first pupil had got right to the heart of the techniques of the critical evaluation of evidence by seeking to identify who had produced the source and why. The second had made a leap in his imagination to another visual source on a similar theme produced some 900 years later.

An appreciation of change and continuity

Now some can live in luxury while others weep in woe;
There's very pretty difference now and a century ago.
The world will shortly move by steam, it may appear so strange,
So you must all acknowledge that England wants a change.
('The State of Great Britain or a Touch at the Times' – a broadsheet of the 1840s)

An appreciation of change and continuity means an awareness that the past is different from the present but that nevertheless we share certain characteristics with our forbears, and that different chronological and geographical circumstances affect methods, alter priorities, and condition attitudes and aspirations. History also demonstrates that change has neither a constant rate nor a consistant direction: developments in technology, warfare, culture, and political and moral attitudes have often been interrupted by bewildering bursts of rapidly accelerating change.
A boy in the top class of a primary school was trying to find out about changes in the cost of living. To do so

he was comparing a photocopy of an inventory of household goods of the 1870s with its values attached, with the price of the same articles in an illustrated catalogue of a departmental store, issued in the 1900s, and with current prices in the shops.

What this example illustrates is that, however complex the ideas of change and continuity may be, in a simple form they are accessible even to young children.

An understanding of cause

It is an error to confuse facts with causes, and to suppose that the historian can explain all by confining his interests to what 'happened'. HUGH TREVOR-ROPER

Pupils are often presented with, or already hold, simple causal explanations for events: 'because they are rich', 'because she was in love', 'because they were Catholics', 'because they were black'. Genuinely historical explanations, however, are necessarily tentative, demand qualifications and must admit to exceptions. Events may have a multiplicity of causes, and historical explanation seeks to reveal the link between the occasion and the underlying trends or tensions. Consecutive events do not inevitably have a causal relationship. Many are precipitated by factors neither sought nor anticipated by the participants.

These are difficult connections to make, but there is evidence that they are within the capacity of many pupils of a wide range of ability.

Historical empathy

Historical imagination is a loyal and indispensable servant of truth that has nothing in common with fantasy or caprice. ADOLFO GILLY

Historical empathy is the ability to enter into some informed appreciation

of the predicaments or points of view of other people in the past. It depends on an imaginative interpretation of evidence and, in particular, on an ability to be aware of anachronism and to imagine historical circumstances the outcome of which could not be known at the time. Empathizing is not the same as identifying with, still less sympathising with, people in the past; it is simply a word used to describe the imagination working on evidence, attempting to enter into a past experience while at the same time remaining outside it.

A class of first year secondary pupils, trying to shoot imaginary neolithic game with appropriate weapons they had made, found that the task was much more difficult than they had imagined and realised that neolithic man was not stupid.

Historical empathy should be part of the learning of all pupils across the whole age and ability range. It can often be encouraged by discussion, simulations, role-play, and drama – strategies often found in the best of primary practice. Such activities might pose the question, for example, why William of Normandy still decided to cross the Channel in the autumn of 1066, despite the threat of equinoctial gales, knowing that he might face a powerful and effective Saxon army but unaware of its forced march from the North.

An ability to pose historical questions

The one real object of education is to leave a man in the condition of continually asking questions. BISHOP CREIGHTON.

The ability to ask questions and to make informed judgements is the key to historical knowledge. 'How do I know that this is true?', 'What was it like to be . . .?', 'What would I have done if . . .?' are all crucial historical questions. They are also of considerable social importance. They will enable pupils not only to understand their heritage and share it with others but also to develop their individual awareness and give them some help towards coming to terms with the present.

A sense of chronology and time

The aim of history, I believe, is to understand men both as individuals and in their social relationships in time. J H PLUMB

The question of children's sense of time worries many teachers who see it as a stumbling block in the development of historical understanding. However, the ability to conceive of the duration of historical time and of the difference, for example, between 500 years and 2,000 years is difficult not only for the young but for most adults too. It may be more helpful to concentrate less on historical time and more on an understanding of historical chronology, which is perhaps easier to identify and capable of being acquired by young children. It provides a structure that enables children to make sense of what might otherwise be a kaleidoscope of events.

The distinction between 'once upon a time' stories and those of history can be made by very young children. When children move from infant to junior classes, they often have the beginnings of a chronological framework that enables them to put objects or pictures into correct sequence. The work of John and Margaret West in the Midlands has demonstrated this ability very clearly.* A class of 6 year olds, for example, when given a box of flints, without any explanation as to what they were, not only identified them correctly, but were able to put them in a chronological order based on the simple hypothesis that the flint that cut best was probably made later. There is no reason why children, by the time they leave primary schools, should not have acquired a chronological structure that enables them to use such terms as 'Stone Age', 'Greek and Roman', 'Medieval', 'Tudor', 'Victorian', and 'recent' correctly. Thus, at least by the early years of secondary education, most pupils can acquire a framework that enables them to sequence historical stories and materials in a general way, although it will have gaps that gradually have to be filled in as their experience is extended.

The experience and observation of teachers suggest that time charts supply a useful means of helping children to acquire a chronological scheme and make more sense of what they have experienced, particularly if they include some reference to events within the memory of the child and his or her family. An understanding of chronology can also be developed if it can be related to objects, places and pictures, so that stories and events are differentiated not only by dates but also, for example, by dress, weapons, forms of transport, or buildings. Museum tables are found in first and junior schools. Not only can they supply concrete evidence of historical chronology but they can be related to the development of skills of collection and categorisation, and offer opportunities to pose questions and develop hypotheses. A class looking at a Victorian photograph of a familiar site can be asked: 'Do you think that the photographer and the people in this photograph are still alive? What is different? What is the same?'. Such questions not only develop a sense of chronology but relate it to the concepts of 'continuity' and of 'change' and help to identify anachronism.

Language and history

History teaching can give pupils up to the age of 16 opportunities to develop their use of language. They can discuss, ask questions, defend a case, make hypotheses, analogies and comparisons, argue and extrapolate. They must marshal and evaluate evidence. They can interview people, play roles, and imaginatively reconstruct the past. Language is the most important of the media through which pupils can express their enthusiasms.

*West, John and West, Margaret. *History 7–13 (guidelines, structures and resources) with 50 classroom examples.* Dudley: Dudley Teachers' Centre, 1981.

2 Lindow Man – "Pete Marsh"

3 War time evacuees

If the pupils' vocabulary and handling of the mechanics of language are to develop and grow, the teacher must accept as a starting point in that process the stage each individual child has reached. This acceptance is essential because the development of the ability to handle language has to come from within the pupils themselves; it cannot be imposed from without. They have to feel comfortable with the language they use and the way in which they use it. They feel uncertain and uncomfortable if they are forced to adopt the language and vocabulary of others and, paradoxically, rather than seeking understanding, may look for security in dictated notes and wholesale copying from the textbook.

The work of one mixed ability class of 13 and 14 year olds, done in a double period of 80 minutes, illustrates something of the variety of language training that can take place within a single class and, in particular, the opportunity it can give to study the important problem of emotive language. The teacher and the pupils discussed the Pilgrimage of Grace and looked at some of the documentary evidence about its progress and impact. The class was then divided into two groups. One group wrote a brief account of Aske's uprising from the point of view of supporters of his cause; the other wrote an account from the point of view of opponents of the

Pilgrimage and supporters of Henry VIII. Individual pupils were then selected to read out what they had written. The less able as well as the more able were asked to contribute. Afterwards, the teacher guided the class discussion so that the pupils would identify the emotive words that had been used for and against the rebellion – though Aske's supporters would not accept that it was a rebellion! These 'loaded' words were written on the blackboard and a lively discussion then took place about exactly what their role had been. The pupils were then given documentary extracts from the visitations to the monasteries. They were asked to consider how objective the commissioners had been in their investigations. Once again the discussion was a lively one – some pupils arguing that certain words were 'loaded', others just as fiercely that they were not. The class also considered the likely effect of the use of such words in a situation of that kind. The discussion included a thorough examination of the nature of bias before the pupils were set homework, asking them to make up their minds about the visitation and to use the documentary evidence to support their conclusions.

History involves an ability to see the meanings and implications of language used by people in other times and circumstances. It is particularly concerned with the detection of bias.

This not only involves an understanding of the historical circumstances in which a document was written and the motives of its author but some appreciation of emotive and figurative language. It involves an appreciation of the fact that many words are not objective but contain value judgements, for example:

execution	courageous
hordes	foolhardy
swamped	extremist
noble	nationalism
dissenter	patriotism
rebel	terrorist
revolutionary	freedom-fighter

Language, too, has its own history. Words can retain their form but change their meaning or become variously associated with new ideas and attitudes. The thoughts of people in other ages may only be appreciated if these changes in meaning and use are also appreciated.

Writing a narrative is a complex but necessary activity for pupils, and it depends on grasping such basic matters as sentence construction, punctuation, tense, paragraphs, and the use of conjunctions. This understanding does not occur in isolation; it goes hand in hand with the successful development of the ordering and expressing of ideas. An effective narrative depends not only on selecting and highlighting relevant factors but on excluding extraneous ones and on handling subplots while developing the main plot. It must be concerned with the understanding and expression of cause and consequence.

History calls for a range of language skills and competencies and provides a great range of opportunities for pupils to develop their potential in understanding and using language. If these opportunities are to be fully exploited, history can offer a richer diet than dictated or copied notes, or the excessive use of worksheets that inhibit rather than extend pupil's language skills. The study of history contributes to the development of language. The more confident and sensitive use of language can make pupils better historians.

History can introduce young children*, as much as it can older pupils, to some understanding of what is meant by 'real' and 'true' in human affairs. Its raw material is evidence of the past and raises questions such as 'How do we know that this really happened?', or 'How can we tell what it really would have been like to live in a Stone Age village?'. Objects, pictures, and stories told by witnesses and handed down through the generations are the materials that leads us to decide what is real about the past. Children often find these questions fascinating, but they need to become accustomed to asking them if their understanding of human affairs is to develop.

A class of 6 year olds had been encouraged to bring to school objects they had found in their gardens: flints, broken china, and bones. The teacher

enlisted the local museum curator and it soon became automatic for the children to bring other finds to school for identification. The habit of asking about things, where they came from and what happened at the time they were used, led the children to ask their parents and grandparents about life in the area during the last war and when they were children. Their discoveries were incorporated into a scrapbook of vivid writing and illustrations. These children were developing a lively curiosity and were acquiring a sense of who to ask and where to look for answers.

Stories and myths

More than this, history can make significant contributions to children's moral understanding. Their own reactions of approval and disapproval to stories and characters are intuitive, and they often adopt a simple morality that clearly differentiates between good and evil, heroes and villains. Stories of great lives as well as those of ordinary people can begin to show the dilemmas and constraints that people faced as a result of the limitations of their knowledge, technology, wealth, and geographical environment. Heroes and villains will remain, but history teaching can begin to encourage children to see qualities and shortcomings as matters for speculation and discussion, as they consider some of the stories of people in the past. Pupils in this age group can begin to relate judgements about people to evidence and to identify with the

predicaments and points of view of others.

Stories can be used to lead children more and more towards a grasp of historical reality. The stories may not necessarily be wholly true but will be authentic – inasmuch as anachronisms have been eliminated. For example, a story might be of an imagined but typical soldier in the army of Julius Caesar, but the details of his way of life, dress and weapons would be real in the sense of their being authentic. Such stories can help children to identify the ways in which the past differs from the now and those in which it is the same. Their telling can be supported by the handling of objects from the period or by looking at pictures either from, or representative of it.

It is often difficult to draw a distinction between myths and stories concerned with real people. Clearly, the great myths of Europe, North America, Africa, and Asia are likely to play an important part in the experience of young children. However, teachers can discuss stories and myths using phrases such as 'Did this really happen?', 'Why was this story told?', and 'How can we tell whether this is true?'. They might also help children to understand that many myths helped people in the past make sense out of incomprehensible and frequently disastrous natural events and to personalise their gods.

*The emphasis of this section is on pupils ages 5 to 8. Inevitably any age distinction is bound to be arbitrary and unhelpfully precise. Pupils' knowledge of history and experience of human behaviour varies considerably and can never tidily be related to precise chronological ages.

As well as being told stories, children can be encouraged to handle objects, look at pictures, listen, talk, paint, model and act. When children are looking at objects or pictures from the past, they should be prompted to ask 'What is it?', 'What was it for?', 'Who made it and why?', 'Who wanted it and why?', 'What difference did it make to people's lives?', and 'What does this tell us about life in the past?'. At the same time the basic vocabulary of chronology and time can gradually be introduced – for example, such words and phrases as 'then', 'now', 'long ago', 'during', 'before', 'afterwards', 'during my lifetime', and 'when my grandfather was a little boy'. A beginning can be made on the acquisition of an understanding of chronology either by telling stories in sequence or by picturing on a time-chart the historical people who figured in such stories. Such a chart needs a minimum of fixed points and is completed gradually with the children producing pictures of the stories they have heard, or ordering the objects they have collected and putting them on the chart in chronological sequence. Some sense of the scale of historical time spans can be established by including incidents from the lives of pupils and their families.

For these younger pupils, it is likely that much of the curriculum will be taught by the same class teacher. Stories and other activities will be a common vehicle for developing, for example, language, number, understanding of the environment and the past, and for stimulating a variety of work in art and craft, music, movement and drama, which in turn may stimulate interesting historical questions and activities. The teacher can seek opportunities to tease out those aspects of the story or activity that are historical.

The following checklist may be helpful to teachers wishing to ensure that there is genuine historical content and development of historical understanding in topics or projects and within interdisciplinary activities.

● Are the stories and enquiries about *people* and what they did? Topics or projects about fossils or dinosaurs, though concerned with the past, are not history as it has been defined in this pamphlet.

● Is there an attempt to ask questions about how and why *changes* occurred?

● Are the stories and activities set in a *chronological framework*? Do they relate to other events that happened about the same time that children already know about? Is there scope for relating the events to children's own experience and that of their families?

● Does the topic *relate to previous work done and to that likely to be done in the future*? If the work is being done in the last years of a first or infant school, is there some attempt to relate it to the work that might be done in the first years of the child's next phase of education?

● Are there opportunities for children to use *historical sources*, eg pictures, objects, and the memories of people who lived at the time?

● Do the knowledge and the experience given to children in the classroom offer the *opportunities to imagine* what it was like to live in another period? Can they begin to detect anachronism?

While history will not necessarily be taught as a separate subject, there should be a planned approach to enable children to acquire historical understanding. There is a distinctness about history and its enquiries and interests that does not apply to science or geography. Aquiring historical understanding is a long process and the contribution that teaching in the 5 to 8 age range can make towards this should not be denied or neglected.

5 Medieval knights

Examples of work

Here are two examples of one term's work.

Example 1

The school is a one-form-entry first school with an age range of 5 to 9. None of the teachers is a trained historian. Many of the children have reading problems. It serves a mining village which once had five pits; when the children were doing the work described in the next paragraph, only one pit survived and that has since closed. The local authority used the village for rehousing in its slum clearance scheme and for settling problem families. The history of the village goes back to at least the twelfth century, and traces of its agricultural character still exist.

The proposal to study the village and to involve the whole school was discussed two terms before the project was launched, and careful planning was a major element in its success. During this period, materials were collected – photographs, maps, directories, and so on – and resource centres, libraries, archives and local people were contacted. Children were encouraged to bring in relevant materials. At first, it was felt that the reception class should not be involved; but the children insisted, and it was decided that they should take the theme: 'Old and New'. This proved to be a valuable exercise, raising such questions as, 'How do you know it is old?' and 'How old is it?', and bringing in the concept of change. The rest of the project was divided into five main topics: farming, buildings, the development of the village, the school, and mining.

6 and 7 year old children tackled farming. They visited a farm and were fascinated by the nineteenth-century gin-gang by which horses drove the farm machinery, and by the fact that the farmhouse was over 200 years old. They traced the changes in the field boundaries by comparing the tithe map, the first edition of the 6-inch Ordnance Survey map and the current 6-inch Ordnance Survey map. They gleaned much of the farm's history by questioning the farmer.

The village study was undertaken by 7 and 8 year olds. They used old maps and dated stones to identify the ages of the buildings. They worked on directories, and on old photographs and postcards, as well as interviewing people, to build up their picture of the village in the past. The discovery that a hoard of Roman coins had been found there in 1812, and had since disappeared, led to much excitement and speculation as to how it had got there and where it had gone.

Most of the children in the top class, aged 8 and 9, worked on the mining history of the village. They used facsimile documents, maps and pictures, old photographs, artefacts and oral evidence. They visited the sites of the mines, although they were not allowed underground. A separate village had grown up around one of the mines, but when the children visited the site no vestige of the village remained: this again caused much speculation, reference to old maps, and imaginative reconstruction based on evidence. Five children from this class undertook a study of the history of their school, referring to the log books, old exercise books and archive materials,

and talking to former pupils. A visit to the original school building brought home to them the overcrowding and other marked differences in conditions then and now.

The whole project showed that children of this age range, some with learning difficulties and none of them privileged, were able to work with a variety of historical sources, to ask historical questions, to speculate on historical problems, to build up an historical picture, and to be fascinated by history. They shared their enjoyment with the rest of the village by mounting an exhibition and giving its visitors guided tours.

Example 2

A group of able children aged from 6 to 10 in an East Anglian primary school were also studying their locality. They were using nineteenth-century maps – including a huge blow-up on the classroom wall of an 1886 Ordnance Survey map of the district census returns – photocopies of directories of the 1880s and 1890s, old photographs, and a captive 80 year old who was putting his memories on to cassette. The results included a graphical record of birthplaces, occupations and family size in certain streets, and a large collage of costumes of the 1880s. The children had also visited the same streets, questioned the 80 year old, and annotated the enlarged map.

There are many lessons to be learnt from these two schools, not the least being that a firm foundation can be built before a child is 9, and that, if it is firmly built on, older children can do much more advanced work than they are often considered capable of.

Before the age of 8, the foundations for historical understanding can be laid. Between the ages of 8 and 16, children may begin to move to more sophisticated stages of historical understanding. They can begin to structure their experience as they develop an understanding of concepts of reality, historical chronology, place, change and causation. Attitudes and interests that were implicit when they were younger begin to emerge more clearly, and teachers can begin to organise their teaching and their pupils' learning around them. Pupils can identify more precisely the differences between the present and the past and find them fascinating, particularly the details of 'how they used to live then'. They can now raise more spontaneously questions such as 'Is it true?' and 'How do we know?'. However, they may still need a story that moves from its beginning to its conclusion in a narrative that provides its own explanation. As children mature, discussion and writing can encourage them to explore more complex narratives, to analyse people's motives, and to pose their own hypotheses about why people acted as they did. They can begin to be aware of the complexity of human behaviour and the provisional nature of historical statements.

For most pupils up to the age of 11 – indeed, for some up to the age of 13 or even 14 – history will still be taught by class teachers, many of whom will not be history specialists. Such arrangements often have considerable social benefits and can offer opportunities to relate the pupils'

6 'Your Country Needs You' Kitchener recruiting poster

7 US recruiting poster

8 German poster

study of the past to their experiences and to other subjects. However, this places a responsibility for guidance and in-service training on those history specialists who *are* in the schools. In many primary and middle schools there may be only one member of staff with any specialist experience of teaching history, in some none at all.

The HMI primary survey[1] suggested

that one factor contributing to much superficial work in history was lack of planning. Therefore it is important for primary and middle schools to have a teacher with a designated responsibility for history to act as a consultant for the whole staff; such a teacher should not only write the scheme of work for

[1] *Primary education in England: a survey by HM Inspectors of Schools.* HMSO, 1978.

history, or that part of the curriculum containing it, and regularly advise their colleagues, but also on occasions teach in classes other than their own. In many schools there are of course no such specialist teachers. Necessary support may be given by the headteacher, supported by local education authority advisers.

Continuity

Establishing effective continuity between the primary and secondary phases and progression in teaching and learning from 5 to 16 is not easy. A secondary school may draw its pupils from many primary schools, some of which may have curricular policies and social characteristics that make them very different both from the secondary school and from other primary schools in the areas. Teachers may feel that allowing their colleagues in other schools to exert an influence, however benign, on their curriculum is to surrender some of their autonomy. Nevertheless, now that schools are becoming increasingly accountable to the communities they serve, and the aims and objectives of the curriculum are now more open to public scrutiny, teachers in different schools will be expected jointly to ensure that pupils, as they move upwards through the educational system, will benefit from a more cohesive curriculum.

Although there is a strong case for all pupils continuing history up to the age of 16, it is likely to remain an option at 14 in most schools. While no overall and precise statistics are available, it seems that about 50 per cent of pupils cease to study history at this age. This break should serve as a constant reminder that the syllabus for pupils aged 8 to 14 ought not only to be coherent but should have a comprehensible terminal point. Consequently, whatever the particular local arrangement with the school age ranges, or arrangements for maintaining curricular continuity across them, it is particularly important to coordinate studies in history over the

years from 8 to 14. This inevitably means cooperation between primary, middle or secondary schools. Such links are not easy to organise and they involve time. An exchange of syllabuses between schools, and the production of LEA guidelines for history, can be useful steps leading to discussion of skills, content and the use of local resources. At least, purposeless repetition of content might then be avoided.

The establishment of such links, although ultimately the responsibility of head teachers, will be part of the role of heads of departments and of consultants in primary and middle schools. The links often involve unfamiliar and sometimes delicate professional relationships. An LEA policy, supported by its advisory staff, can have a crucial role in establishing effective liaison.

The same arguments apply to the inclusion of history in the curriculum for pupils of 8 or above as they do for pupils aged from 5 to 8, though a further argument for the value of history emerges more clearly. History is one of the most important means of helping young people to understand the world into which they have been born. It involves learning not only about the immediate environment of village, town or city, but also about the wider national society with its particular institutions, traditions and problems, and the international world connections that have affected all societies.

Developing skills

Between the ages of 8 and 14, both general study skills and specific 'historical skills', some of which younger children may have begun to develop, ought now to be explicitly stated and pupils encouraged to practise them.

They are:

General skills

● the ability to *locate information* from resources of all kinds, eg books, maps,

pictures, films, statistics and diagrams, objects, buildings, the memories of people;

● the ability to *observe, listen, and record*;

● the ability to *communicate:* to write clearly in a variety of forms, to argue a case, orally and on paper, to participate in discussions;

● skills of *translation:* the ability to express ideas in a form different from the original, eg putting into written form information contained in graphs, statistics and pictures, to translate archaic literary styles into contemporary language;

● skills of *analysis and synthesis:* the ability to select and organise information, pose and test hypotheses, ask appropriate questions, construct narratives, write notes and essays;

● the ability to *recall information*.

Skills of history

● the ability to use *chronological conventions* and put events in *sequence*;

● the ability to use *historical evidence*, ie the skill of relating statements about people or groups of people to evidence and its critical evaluation, including the detection of bias; the realization that historical statements are tentative and provisional; some familiarity with the range and variety of evidence; an ability to distinguish between primary and secondary sources;

● the ability to make *empathetic judgements*, ie to enter into some informed appreciation of the predicaments and points of view of other people in the past;

● the ability to use *historical concepts and ideas*. A suggested list of terms pupils should be familiar with by the time they may leave school at the age of 16 is given on page 15.

The development of these skills must be related both to cultivating an awareness of what are appropriate historical questions to ask (guidance for which is given in Section 6) and to establishing a history syllabus within which they can be exercised.

What should pupils aged 16 know and be able to do better than they could at the age of 11, or 8, or 5? A scheme of work[1] is a plan for answering these questions. But it also gives some indication as to *how* the plan is to be achieved and of how to test its success, or failure. And so it includes references to suitable resources, teaching styles and forms of assessment. It is also an important working document, ensuring that learning about the past relates not only to the levels of historical understanding and knowledge of pupils but also, as far as is possible, to the variety of their school experience. A scheme of work for history should therefore be part of a curriculum that is coherent and makes sense to children as they move upwards through the school system. Further, as part of a mobile population, pupils often move from one local education authority to another. Ideally their experience of history should be free from ungainly and arbitrary gaps, repetitions, and contradictions.

A checklist of questions such as the following can help to evaluate a scheme of work:

● What are the general aims of the scheme and the particular objectives of its different sections?

● What skills, both general and historical, does it seek to develop?

● What historical concepts and ideas[2] does it want pupils to understand and use?

● Do the concepts and ideas relate to the development of children's understanding and the extent of their knowledge?

● Are they listed in some order of difficulty and complexity, ie does the scheme aim to develop progression in children's learning?

● Are appropriate teaching methods being considered, eg writing, discussion, role-play, painting, modelling, drama, group or individual projects?

● What resources are suitable and *available*, eg the knowledge and experience of teachers, printed material, audio-visual aids, resources outside the school – sites, museums, archives, loan services of public libraries? Are written and oral resources couched in suitably accessible language?

● How does the teacher know that the objectives are being achieved, ie what are the assessment techniques, marking policies, school examinations, class tests, class discussion, homework?

● Since the whole of history cannot be taught, what content is going to be studied, what are the criteria for its selection, and does that content help to develop skills, concepts and ideas?

Content and function

Not to know what took place before you were born is to remain forever a child. CICERO

History teachers, and those who offer them advice, are often accused of being evasive about content and told that their pupils are ignorant of key events in the past. It is not an unreasonable charge if pupils appear to know little after years of formal history teaching. For many parents, employers, and non-historians in schools, the acquisition of historical content is part of their own experience and an aspect of the subject that is both comprehensible and accessible. Historical content can begin to make an effective case for the subject. Of course, a scheme of work that depends entirely on content and ignores concepts and skills seriously threatens its effectiveness, but to write such a scheme without justifying the choice of content would diminish its impact.

Our roots as individuals lie in the history of our families and, possibly, in that of our locality. Our schools share some of the same roots. All pupils have in common the country in which they live and have characteristics moulded in part of its past. But in a multicultural society and an interdependent world, a history syllabus cannot ignore countries beyond these islands and Europe. Thus, faced with an environment that ranges from the parish pump to spaceships, the selection of content is a daunting task. But it cannot be tackled unless historians are able to define not only the nature of history but its functions. This may suggest an uncomfortably instrumentalist

[1]A scheme of work is the statement of the aims, objectives, skills, content, methods of teaching and assessment and resources. A syllabus is the statement of the content to be included in the scheme of work.

[2]See pages 14 and 15.

approach to the subject, but it is not inconsistent either with the study of the past as an end in itself or as a source of personal satisfaction.

Life, leisure and work

Misunderstanding of the present is the inevitable consequence of ignorance of the past. But a man may wear himself out just as fruitlessly in seeking to understand the past, if he is totally ignorant of the present. MARC BLOCH

History is part of the process through which a society shares a common memory of the past of the country in which all pupils live. This is heritage history, and to some this might be outmoded; to others, it will be a welcome means to developing a sense of informed but critical pride in their country. But however this aspect of the subject is applied and interpreted by individuals – and it is no task of history teachers to decide that in advance for their pupils – there is considerable value in a society's shared recognitions and memories. Professor Marwick challenges us to imagine what everyday life would be like in a society in which no one knew any history. 'Imagination boggles, because it is only through knowledge of its history that a society can have knowledge of itself. As a man without memory and self-knowledge is a man adrift, so a society without memory (or, more correctly, without recollection) and self-knowledge would be a society adrift'.[1]

History contributes to a preparation for leisure. This view needs to be stated confidently and without defensiveness. Whatever future prospects of employment hold for young people, they are likely to spend far less of their time actually at work. The introduction to this book referred to the multitude of activities that are evidence of the interest in the past pursued as a leisure activity. History teaching is part of its professional underpinning and contributes significantly to stimulating and strengthening this interest.

History is one of the most important means of decreasing our ignorance and diminishing our misunderstanding of the **contemporary world** by placing it in its historical context of change and evolution.

History, with a few exceptions for some careers, cannot claim to be a vocational subject. Nevertheless, a subject that insists on the critical evaluation of evidence – written, pictorial, and statistical – and encourages the analysis of problems and the communication of ideas, not only contributes to pupils' general education but develops skills and perceptions that increase the **employability** of young people.

Finally, history is a crucial part of the **personal development** of its students, first, because our knowledge of what we are as individuals and members of groups, and our ability to anticipate and aspire to what we might become, depends on the knowledge and understanding of what we have been. Second, our development as moral individuals depends in part on the historian's insistence that the judgements of individuals and groups should be based on evidence, and on constant opportunities to understand the predicaments and attitudes of other people. History helps its students living in an open society to decide between alternative attitudes and courses of action with some degree of knowledge, understanding and competence. History also satisfies our innate curiosity to look for answers to the questions 'why' and 'how' and stimulates us to go on asking them.

How do we select?

To list the purposes of history teaching merely serves to build up alarmingly the number of periods and topics possible for study. To propose a syllabus that, apparently, includes the whole of British history, not forgetting that of the locality of the school, and of the rest of the world, covering a time span up to the present, would be unhelpful. How then *do* we select content? Two

contrasted responses are often given. One says that, provided the skills are correctly identified and effectively taught, the content does not matter. The other asserts that there are major themes and periods in history that no young person should leave school without having studied – for example, the Tudors, the English Civil War, the Industrial Revolution, the Russian Revolution, and so on. The difficulty with the first answer is that skills are unlikely to be acquired, let alone effectively applied, unless they are related to content that has some inherent interest and appears to relate to the lives of the pupils. Nor is it an approach, as we have suggested, likely to make a persuasive case for history to others. The question of selection is in fact evaded, not answered. On the other hand, the argument that searches for an agreed list of major themes and great lives reflects the views of many people that it would indeed be regrettable if children left school unaware of certain key issues and events, firmly based on knowledge. The problem here is that in our multicultural society and in an interdependent world, it is easier to add to the list of key periods and topics than to subtract. Resulting syllabuses bulge with importance and suffocate with priorities. Thus this point of view merely restates the problem in other terms and does not resolve it.

But there are criteria – indeed, necessary conditions – related to location, key issues in contemporary society, concepts and skills that offer a basis for rational selection.

Location

The periods a particular school chooses could more often be affected, by the resources available outside the school and need not be wholly controlled, as they so often are, by the resources in the history stock cupboard and the school library. How near is a museum or a county archive? Does either have education officers to support the use of

[1]Marwick, Arthur. *The nature of history.* Macmillan, 1970.

artefacts and documents in schools? Is there a parish church? Is it medieval or high Victorian Gothic? Is there a Roman villa, a castle, or an eighteenth-century country house? Or is there a great Victorian railway terminus or a Second World War fighter station near the school? Are there themes in our past that still inform the lives of the pupils within a particular school? A primary school in Wiltshire, for example, would ignore its environment and waste accessible resources if it took no notice of pre-history or the agricultural revolution. Other schools in, say, Shropshire or the West Midlands, for similar reasons, would be foolish to ignore industrial history. More attention might well be given to the Vikings in York than in Exeter. It would be odd to see the English Civil War ignored in Oxfordshire, or the effect of the expansion of the railways

on English society in schools in Stockton, St. Helens, or Islington. Almost certainly, the particular locality of the school not only provides opportunities for children to become familiar with a variety of evidence and to learn something about their own family roots, but to relate the history of their village or town to great national events such as the Norman Conquest, the Wars of the Roses, the General Strike or the Second World War.

Contemporary society

Again, general statements of aims offer no helpful criteria for selection. *What* themes and problems do we want to help your people understand? Any list is bound to be arbitrary, to reflect our values and current preoccupations, and thus to be open to challenge and debate.

But teachers have to take just such difficult decisions. The following themes are neither exclusive, nor necessarily authoritative:

● The growth of towns and cities and the consequent demographic changes in our world.

● The effect on our lives – political, social, economic, cultural, moral – and on the distribution and nature of employment and leisure of science and technology.

● The issues of an open society that present young people with a range of social, political and moral choices. This means an understanding at least of the evolution of our political institutions and democracy, of religious freedom, and of the development of industrial relations. Such themes might ask: What makes British society distinctive?

9 The coming of the National Grid

What ideals and values do we hold in common, even allowing for our many differences? How were certain values and achievements that others do not have, and we did not always have, brought about, eg freedom of worship, of discussion, of movement, of industrial relations?

• A society in which the status and contributions of women are changing and under increasing re-examination (see pages 29 and 30).

• A multicultural society. This complicated and sensitive area is given further consideration (see pages 30 to 32).

• An internationally interdependent society. Here again it is difficult to give an authoritative list of themes, but it might well include the historical experiences of the United States and the Soviet Union as part of the explanation of their stances and attitudes in the world today, an introduction to the issues of peace and war and to the debate that seeks the means to achieve one and to avoid the other, some historical perspectives on the movements of peoples and the changing global distribution of wealth. Syllabus planners will also have to ask themselves whether these, or other themes, relate to particular regional issues of current importance. Would it not be odd if, in the 1980s, history syllabuses avoided consideration of Irish history or that of the Middle East?

Concepts and ideas as a guide to selection

Historical knowledge includes an understanding of certain ideas and concepts.[1] These are more than glossaries of technical terms; they are aids to categorising, organising, analysing and applying historical information. They can only be understood when they are used in illustrating a variety of different historical circumstances. 'Revolution', for example, is a historical idea. But a simple definition will not help pupils to understand why the word is applied

equally to events in France after 1789, in Russia in 1917, or to the history of industry in later eighteenth century England, or whether it can equally usefully describe events in seventeenth century England. Ideas such as 'left wing', or 'right wing', have their value, but only if pupils begin to appreciate their limitations and the over-simplifications they sometimes suggest.

It is difficult to compile a definitive list of historical concepts and ideas which are held to be necessary conditions for historical understanding. Many terms that young people should have met by the age of 16 are included in the list opposite (Table 1). It is true that particular periods or problems studied will modify the list, but nevertheless there remain three concepts fundamental to all historical study and to which all others relate: *cause, change and evidence*. They must be present, implicitly at least, in the work of the whole age group.

Of course, some pupils will be able to demonstrate by the age of 16 a sound understanding of the meaning of many of the terms on the list and be able to use them explicitly. Others may only be aware of them indirectly by being introduced to events which illustrate them. Many pupils, for example, will never be able, or indeed need, to use terms such as 'oligarchy'. Nevertheless, there is no reason why they cannot understand how a few men ruled the Venetian Republic, or a small group administers their school.

But if many concepts and ideas cannot explicitly be understood by all pupils, they remain among the criteria that can help teachers to select periods or particular themes within periods. If teachers take the development of concepts and ideas seriously, even content-dominated syllabuses have something to offer. For example, children learn about dozens of wars but rarely about the phenomenon of war. Or, they learn about machines, ships, pyramids, railways and so on, but not about the phenomenon of technology or its impact on people's lives. If a history teacher aims to develop an

understanding of 'democracy', it suggests a syllabus that might include Magna Carta and Simon de Montfort (if only to correct some myths), the English Civil War and the growth of Parliamentary democracy, and trade unionism in the nineteenth and twentieth centuries; it might also include the American War of Independence. If the aim is to establish the important distinction between 'power' and 'authority', it might, for example, suggest certain themes to emphasise in teaching the history of sixteenth century Europe. The Age of the Explorers and the history of the British Empire can offer opportunities to develop an understanding of such ideas as 'imperialism', 'colonialism', 'culture', and 'civilisation'. On the other hand, the study of the first and second Industrial Revolutions can help not only to examine the relationship between 'change', 'progress' and 'improvement', but also to draw the important distinction between 'science' and 'technology'.

Criteria of skills

General skills of study, and specifically historical skills (which are the essence of the subject), offer a further group of criteria for the selection of content. If, for example, one objective in history teaching is to give pupils the skills of working independently and effectively in a library, then only those periods of history that are adequately represented on the library shelves can be selected. If another objective is to give young people an opportunity to develop skills of evaluating a range of primary source material – newspapers, statistics, old photographs, the memories of old people, street names, field patterns – then the history of an area and a time

---

[1]The distinction employed here is between **concepts** such as cause and effect, continuity and change, or evidence by means of which we attempt to identify relationships between events, organise the past into recognisable patterns or determine what is to count as a valid historical statement; and **ideas** such as revolution, feudal, state and renaissance, by means of which we seek to categorise past events by reference to certain agreed features.

when these sources are accessible have to be chosen. Such an objective is one of the rationales for studying the locality, including its recent past.

Table 2 on pages 18 and 19 summarises historical and general skills and relates them to children's learning ages.

Evaluating the syllabus

The following questions can be used as a basis for evaluating the content in a history scheme of work. Answers will, almost certainly, reveal imbalances and identify gaps.

• Does the history syllabus include some periods of national history?

• Does the syllabus offer opportunities to learn something about the achievements of cultures within and outside Europe? Do these opportunities relate to the issues of an interdependent world and a multicultural society?

• Does the syllabus make any contribution to the understanding of the contemporary world by putting it in its historical context, local as well as national?

• Does the study of the locality help towards developing some understanding of pupils' own roots and environment?

• Does the study of the locality link its issues to those of the nation and the world beyond?

• Does a study of these periods help pupils towards an understanding of the complicated relationship between political, social, economic, technical and cultural aspects of society?

• As history is concerned with change and continuity through time, are the themes chosen of sufficient chronological length to illustrate these concepts?

• Does the syllabus help young people towards an understanding of why things are as they are, that things have not always been so, and that they will not necessarily always continue to be so?

No history syllabus exists without considerable gaps in content.

Compromises and sacrifices always have to be made. However, this checklist of questions may help ensure that these are planned and explicit rather than arbitrary and concealed.

If the content of history syllabuses inevitably leaves considerable and sometimes unexplained gaps, coherence and a sense of chronology can be threatened. Nevertheless pupils should be able to fit a diversity of periods and events into some kind of framework, perhaps in the form of a 'timeline', built up during a pupil's school career, so as to define the chronological relationship of these events and their relative distance from the present. Such a timeline could become part of what has been termed 'a map of the past'. It would locate references not only to those periods and lives studied in detail but also to those receiving only cursory treatment. The knowledge and understanding of the events thus located would vary considerably, but understanding a map of the world does not mean equal knowledge of, say, the geography of Australia and that of Western Europe. It does, however, contain a skeleton of basic information, relates places to each other and establishes a sense of scale. Similarly a 'map of the past' could not only provide pupils with a shared framework of knowledge but also serve as a reminder that people's lives and great occasions do not take place in isolation or out of context. It could also act as a systematic reminder that shared recognitions and memories help give communities – national, cultural, class – a claim to identity.

The concepts listed in Table 1 can act as the starting point of a discussion on what a map might contain. But could there ever be agreement on the contents? Probably not, if we seek one single definitive map or framework – although the kind of approach shown in Framework 1 of Appendix 2 might command a fairly wide acceptance. Some teachers, however, may challenge its adequacy and prefer Frameworks 2 or 3.

Table 1: Concepts and ideas commonly used in history teaching with pupils up to the age of 16.

administration	international
agrarian	king/queen
anachronism	labour
anarchism	law
ancient	left-wing
archaeology	legal
aristocratic	liberal
authority/	marxist
authoritarian	medieval
bias	modern
bishop	monarchy
bourgeois	motive
capital	myth
capitalism	nation
Catholic	noble
civilisation	oligarchy
class	parliament
classical	peasants
commonwealth	policy
colony/	political
colonialism	power
communist	prehistory
conclusion	primary source
conservative	progress
constitution	propaganda
continuity	proletariat
conversion	protestant
crusade	radical
culture	reaction
cause	rebellion
change	reform
democratic	religion
development	renaissance
dictator	republic
diplomatic	revolution
economic	right-wing
emperor/empress	ruler
empire	secular
evidence	secondary source
fascist	science
feudal	social
frontier	socialist
government	society
hero/heroine	state
humanist	technology
hypothesis	treaty
imperialism	war
industrial	welfare (state)
inference	

6 PROGRESSION AND PEDAGOGY

Should the learning of pupils aged 16 be any more advanced than the learning of pupils aged 11, or even 8? In what way are pupils at the age of 10 involved in activities that are more demanding than those experienced by pupils aged 7 and 8? To pose those questions to teachers of physical education, metalwork, music, French, or mathematics would appear odd, even eccentric. But many history teachers would have to admit that the main difference between pupils learning history at the age of 16 and those at the age of 11 is that the former have acquired more information. Those teachers in secondary schools able to see pupils studying the past in some primary schools might even be forced to admit that, on occasion, intellectual demands on pupils had actually diminished since they left their primary schools. In too many history classes,

teaching styles continue to be dominated by the need to acquire and remember content. The development of progression and the identification of objectives directly affect teaching and learning.

'Teaching' means the deliberate intention to help others develop and acquire historical knowledge: content, concepts, ideas and skills. 'Learning' is the acquisition and understanding by pupils, through their own efforts of that knowledge, including the processes of location, acquisition, ordering, understanding, application and, where appropriate, memorising. Teaching has to create the intellectual, social, and emotional circumstances that learners need in order to grasp new ideas, develop skills and understand content.

The following questions may help

teachers show pupils how best to handle historical material. They indicate ideas and concepts that will need to be developed in relation to appropriate content. Teachers need to devise a scheme of work that encourages pupils to ask:

- Where and how did people live? How many of them were there? (Settlements and housing.)
- How did the people of the time feed and clothe themselves? (Agriculture, trade, industry.)
- How did people keep themselves alive and well? (Health and industry.)
- What was the available technology? (Industry, transport, weapons, communications.)
- What were the different social groups and their life styles? (Social classes.)
- What did people worship and what values did they try to live by? (Ideas and beliefs.)
- What was their art, music, literature? (Cultural and aesthetic life.)
- Who governed and how, and with what results? (Government and politics.)
- What differences are there between then and now or between different civilisations of the same period?

In addition, there are more specific questions that can be asked of a particular event or series of events.

- What happened, and do we know who was involved?
- When did it happen? (Can I date it or put it in what I know of chronological sequence?)

10 A Macclesfield classroom at the turn of the century

- Why did it happen?

This involves a series of sub-questions:

- What was the immediate cause of the event?
- Were there longer-term causes?
- Were personalities involved whose characteristics helped to bring about the event?
- Were any powerful beliefs, religious or ideological, influencing people at the time?
- How did the various social groups involved view the issues?
- Did any technological developments or material conditions influence the situation?
- How did the strengths or weaknesses of the institutions involved help or hinder?
- What were the results?

Pupils can begin to ask some of these questions before the age of 14, if not perhaps in these words. By the age of 14, when history is still compulsory for most, pupils can be encouraged to ask all of them of the period they have studied. If pupils learn to consider these questions, their historical studies are likely to become more productive, and perhaps more interesting and enjoyable.

Teaching and learning strategies must be diverse if they are to help pupils develop the skills listed in Table 2 on pages 18 and 19, to make them fully aware of the excitement and diversity of the past and if they are to be appropriate for pupils whose abilities and interests vary, even within the same class. At one extreme, there is the lecture where the teacher is the sole source of information, although pupils will still need to deploy skills of listening and recording. At the other, pupils engage in independent learning, regulating their own pace and reflecting their own interests, but are nevertheless still likely to be participating in a programme laid down by the teacher.

Between these two extremes, other strategies include: the provision of guided assignments by the teacher; the supervision of pupils with special learning difficulties or with marked abilities; discussion initiated, led and contributed to by the teacher; discussions led by the pupils with the teacher acting as a guide; cooperative learning by groups of pupils pursuing their own interests with teachers responding to requests for clarification. No one strategy is pre-eminent. But history departments, or teachers of history in primary and middle schools, must monitor the balance and diversity of teaching and learning styles within single classes or during the course of the school term. Without such monitoring, progression, with its pace and timing appropriate for all pupils, cannot be established and measured.

However, neither the pursuit of objectives nor the deployment of teaching and learning strategies can adhere to a too rigid format. Although individual historical skills are sequential in that they contain steps of increasing difficulty, teachers know that pupils often leapfrog, sometimes quite unpredictably, intermediate processes to demonstrate skills at an unexpectedly advanced level. Thus lesson plans and hierarchies of objectives interpreted too rigidly can inhibit the enthusiasms and interests of pupils and of teachers, stifle inventiveness and the expression of opinion, and fail to exploit the experience that all pupils can bring to a history lesson.

Table 2 that follows implies an overall strategy and a general programme rather than prescriptive tactics or a precise menu. It suggests one way of grouping historical objectives and indicates how the various stages in their achievement can be recognised. They have been tried out in a number of schools with classes of average ability in each of the age ranges, although the ages are best seen as intellectual rather than chronological. In many classes, some pupils will be able to attempt harder tasks on the matrix than the majority. Others may not have proceeded so far. The objectives remain broad and general because they have to be. If the matrix is used sensibly, it can help teachers guide their pupils to an understanding of the underlying pattern and purpose of their learning. If classroom strategies are varied and balanced, these skills and ideas will serve pupils as well as adults in weighing evidence, making informed judgements and deriving pleasure and added interest from the events and environments that surround them.

The skills and understandings listed in Table 2 are related to possible teaching strategies and means of assessment. They embody the experience of schools in one LEA and have been used effectively in classrooms.

11 1980s children re-enacting a Victorian schoolroom scene

Table 2 Some objectives for pupil progress in historical skills

	Reference and information-finding skills	Skills in chronology	Language and historical ideas
By the age of 8	Can scan pictures and simple books. Can read simple accounts. Can use page references.	Can use basic vocabulary (eg 'now', 'long ago', 'then', 'before', after'). Begins to understand the chronology of the year (eg seasons); and begins to record on a wall chart sequence of stories heard. Can put some historical pictures and objects in sequence.	Can 'use' terms commonly used in stories of past (eg hero, heroine, king, queen, nobleman, sheriff). Begins to use words such as 'the past', 'myth', 'true'.
By the age of 10	Knows which books supply information (eg topic, encyclopaedias). Can use contents, index and glossaries of books; and can read different passages to select information relevant to a topic. Can use visual sources (eg pictures, filmstrips, slides, artefacts); and oral sources (talk, tape, radio). Can list main points from one or more sources using teachers' questions.	Knows terms BC and AD. Understands 'generation' in a family context. Knows sequence of prehistoric, ancient times, middle ages and modern. Can put a wide range of historical pictures and objects in sequence. Can make a simple individual sequence chart.	Can use an increasing number of terms that arise from topics studied (eg knight, peasant, emperor, bishop). Knows words such as 'history', 'archaeology'.
By the age of 12	Can use a library catalogue (subject). Can read textbooks and topic books in conjunction. Can make more detailed notes under supplied headings using several sources. Can use abbreviations such as eg, ie.	Understands 'century' and how dating by centuries works. Can put dates in correct century. Knows sequence of Roman, Saxon, Viking, Norman, Tudor, Stuart, Victorian. Is aware of some historical period terms (eg Reformation). Can make a time chart using scale.	Can use an increasing number of terms that arise from topics studied (eg keep, lateen, sail). Can use common terms of a greater degree of abstraction (eg ruler, law, subject, parliament).
By the age of 14	Can use more complex cataloguing and retrieval. Can extract information independently from written and pictorial sources. Can make notes in a form that distinguishes main from sub-points.	Is able to put an extensive range of historical pictures and objects in sequence. Can make a time chart that compares developments in contemporary civilisations (eg Iron Age Britain and Ancient Athens, or 16th Century Europe and Aztec/Inca South America). Can make a time chart that records events in different aspects of history (eg war, politics, buildings, costume).	Can use an increasing number of terms that arise from topics studied (eg free trade, invention, protection, imperialist). Can use terms commonly used in historical explanation (eg motive, cause, change, reform, progress, economic, political, social).
By the age of 16	Can summarise. Can ask own questions of information to answer problems. knows how to use and make footnotes and bibliographies (eg in projection work).		Continues to extend knowledge of terms specific to topics studied (eg democracy, liberal, welfare state, fascist, marxist)

Use and analysis of evidence	Empathetic understanding	Asking historical questions	Synthesis and communication using basic ideas
Can describe the main features of concrete evidence of the past (eg pictures, artefacts, buildings) and hypothesise as to their use. Is familiar with the question 'How do we know?'.	Can say, write or draw what they think it felt like in response to some historical story that has been heard.	Begins to become aware of basic historical questions, eg. ● What happened and when? ● Why did it happen? ● How do we know?	Using memory and recall, can describe orally and in writing some past events or story in narrative or dramatic form. Can make a pictorial representation
Can define in simple terms 'source' and 'evidence'. Can understand and make deductions from documentary as well as concrete evidence eg pictures, artefacts). Can describe the main features of simple maps, diagrams or graphs. Increasingly asks the question 'How do we know?'	Can make a simple imaginative reconstruction of a situation in the past and how it appeared to some of the people in it, using the evidence available to draw, model, dramatise, write or tell the story.	Becomes used to asking of any historical period studied question about the main features of everyday life, eg ● When and how did people live and how did they clothe and feed themselves? ● What was the available technology? ● What were the life styles of different social and gender groups? ● What are the differences between now and then?	Can describe orally and in writing some past events or situation recognising *similarities/differences* with today. Can state information in a graph, diagram or map. Can support an account or conclusion with some evidence.
Is aware of variety of historical evidence at different periods of time. Can distinguish between primary and secondary sources; and can understand and make inferences from primary and secondary accounts (text-books, fiction). Can recognise 'gaps' in evidence. Can interpret simple graphical sources.	Can make an imaginative reconstruction that is not anachronistic of a past situation based on several pieces of evidence, including historical fiction, and exploring some of the feelings participants might have had at the time.	Becomes used to asking of any historical period additional questions of increasing difficulty, eg ● Who governed and how and with what results? ● What did they worship and what values did they live by? ● What was their art, music and literature?	Can put together orally and in writing a narrative of past events or situations showing evidence of *continuity* and *change* and indicating simple *causation*. Can make accurate diagrams or maps based on several pieces of evidence.
Can compare two accounts of the same events and note contrasts and similarities. Can recognise that evidence may not be impartial. Can distinguish between fact and opinion. Can begin to interpret simple statistical sources.	Can show understanding of a person's viewpoint within a given historical situation. Can consider the viewpoints of opposing sides and of people for whom they may not feel sympathy.	Begins to analyse historical events by asking questions, eg ● What was the immediate cause? ● Did any long-term cause operate? ● Were there political, economic or religious causes, etc? ● To what extent were personalities important?	Can write an account of some past events in terms of *cause* and *effects* supported by evidence.
Can distinguish relevant and irrelevant evidence. Compare various pieces of evidence and note contradictions and gaps. Can recognise bias and 'propaganda'.	Can identify the extent of choice available to a person in a given situation in the past. Can identify the values and attitudes on which human actions have been based in the past.	Can question different interpretations of past events.	Can write a structured account which, using evidence, argues clearly to a credible conclusion. Can write an analytical account of past events that takes into consideration different interpretations. Can write a longer account using footnotes and bibliographies properly (projects).

7 ASSESSMENT

Assessment is an integral part of the processes of teaching and learning. In some form it needs to be present in every lesson. The teacher's questions to the class and the nature of the responses they provoke provide means of gauging historical understanding, determining whether there has been progression, and diagnosing problems to improve future performance. Beyond this, there will be occasions when it is appropriate to test more formally how well pupils have grasped a given body of work or mastered a particular range of skills. Finally, at the end of their compulsory education, most pupils sit public examinations. Changes in history examinations at 16-plus are likely to assess levels of competence in a range of historical activities. This development, and the wider use of a profile of attainments for pupils from the whole ability range, could throw more emphasis on the performance of pupils throughout their course. These changes carry significant implications for the history department's approach to monitoring and assessment.

Starting points for assessment

Whatever its context, the starting point for effective assessment is 'What do you want these pupils to demonstrate? What tasks will enable them to do so? And how do you measure their performance in them?' At all levels, some history teaching concentrates solely on imparting information. Here assessment is concerned exclusively with testing factual recall – tests that are relatively simple to devise and easy to apply. When, however, the range of teaching objectives is expanded into the mastery of skills or the understanding of ideas and concepts, assessment becomes more difficult and the need to establish guidelines more urgent. In exploring this area certain key issues need to be considered.

It is essential to clarify the nature of the skill to be mastered or the concept to be understood. The processes of teaching, learning and assessment can be effectively linked only if the stages along the road towards attaiment of a given objective are identified and elucidated (as for example in Table 2). Once agreed upon, such stages can then act as criteria by which pupils' progress may be measured.

To attempt to assess at one and the same time pupils' understanding of a wide range of historical skills, ideas and concepts is to risk failure. Paticularly in the early stages it is better to select one skill, concept or idea drawn from a sequence of work, and allow pupils to practise and explore it. When that has been seen to have been undertaken successfully, performance should be recorded and the strategy banked for future use, before moving on to the next order of priority. Table 3 on pages 23 to 26 suggests some of the strategies that might be employed.

The means of assessment must be appropriate both to the age and ability of the pupils and to the particular skill or concept. Tasks may be made unintentionally difficult by the language in which they are couched or the form in which they are presented. Thus the hurdle presented to the pupil may be linguistic rather than conceptual. Similarly, pupils may be able to show in discussion that they have mastered skills that they are not able to demonstrate in a written exercise, or convey ideas through practical work that do not emerge via other forms of activity. Unless they are recognised, such factors will constrain the value and validity of assessment. Equally, questions that merely require the extraction of information from sources are not an appropriate means of assessing the ability to use sources as evidence.

There should be an awareness of the various activities – oral and practical as well as written – that might be employed to judge historical understanding, and of their strengths and limitations.

Although much of learning is achieved through talk and discussion, most assessment still requires a written response. The possibilities of structured and imaginative oral assessment are seldom exploited. Yet appropriate exercises need not be difficult to devise and administer. For example a group of pupils presenting their findings on the causes and consequences of the Black Death could be individually assessed for their command of relevant subject material, their ability to make a case from a particular standpoint and to defend it against counter-arguments, their grasp of the medieval world view, and their understanding of key social and economic ideas. By determining beforehand the elements to be conveyed and the levels of competence expected, judgements can be applied systematically and consistently. Even though such judgements may be partly subjective, they need not be arbitrary.

Practical activities form a significant part of much history teaching particularly, though not exclusively, with younger pupils. These may involve undertaking a fieldwork study, building models, painting pictures, role-play, or drama. All of these activities provide opportunities for assessing how well pupils have acquired historical understanding and skills. Assessment may be of the product (the outcome of the lesson) or of the process. But, if it is to be effective and useful, the criteria for measuring achievement need to be spelt out. What are the skills of effective site investigation? What conclusions might pupils be expected to draw from their investigation? What insights might pupils demonstrate in the process of constructing a model? What sources have they used in determining what people of the past looked like? What questions have they asked about the reliability of their sources? What is to count as authenticity in role-play? Answers to these questions will provide the framework within which assessments can be made.

Within assessment based upon a written response, a wide variety of techniques are now used both by teachers and by examination boards. At one end are devices such as multiple-choice or objective tests which are 'closed' in the sense that they allow of only one correct solution. Although they are attractive because of their reliability and ease of marking, such tests are deceptively difficult to construct and are sometimes of dubious validity. At the other end of the scale are 'open' techniques – essays, investigative assignments or projects – which require pupils to organise material, to ask appropriate questions and to put forward tenable conclusions. In between are tasks that are more or less 'structured' in that varying degrees of guidance are offered to pupils, while still leaving them room for manoeuvre in their responses.

It is worth noting that none of these techniques is necessarily limited in its application. Multiple-choice questions, for example, can be employed to measure the ability to use and analyse documentary sources, as well as to test factual recall – although they may be less revealing than more open approaches.

Whatever techniques or activities form the vehicle for assessment, it is necessary to adopt a systematic approach to determining and recording individual levels of performance.

At each of the stages subsumed within an overall objective, pupils' attainments will vary in terms, for example, of the accuracy with which they are able to place items in chronological sequence; the range of relevant information they are able to extract from sources; the subtlety of the inferences they are able to make; or the consistency with which they are able to employ historical ideas. Establishing levels of performance at a particular stage in a way that furnishes a realistic and valid hierarchy, and in a way that can be reliably applied, is a complex task. But it is essential if grades or marks are to give an indication of what pupils understand and can do, to act as a means of identifying strengths and weaknesses

and to plot pupils' progress. Approached in this way, assessment is concerned with individual performance in relation to specified criteria, rather than in relation to the work of other members of the class. In recording the level of performance, the number of points going to make up the scale of marks or grades is of less importance than that each point should be capable of being translated into a description of achievement. One possible format for a mark book is shown overleaf.

A final issue is the assessment of pupils' attitudes to learning. This is clearly important. Without some assessment of, for example, the extent to which pupils are motivated, it is unlikely that teaching will be effective. Similarly, an assessment of the pupils' interest and enthusiasm can provide a further dimension in evaluating the progress of both the pupil and the department. The willingness of a pupil to contribute to discussion might well form part of the teacher's checklist alongside the criteria for assessing the quality of the contribution. Although specialised techniques for measuring these general attitudes are available it is likely that some simple means of recording them will be of most practical use.

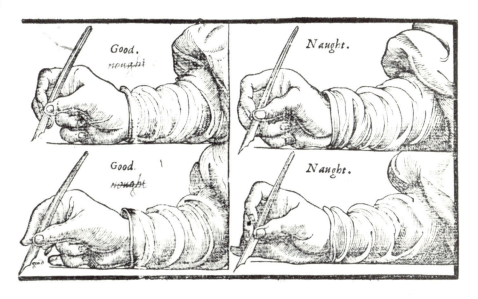

12 "Howe you ought to hold your penne"

ASSESSMENT

Recent thinking on the nature of history teaching presents new challenges, and nowhere more so than in its assessment. The problems may seem daunting, especially when teachers have had to create their own materials and

assessment exercises with little opportunity to draw on the expertise of others. Increasingly, however, LEAs and other bodies are offering guidance on assessment that can be discussed, tried out, modified and developed. The

sharing both of burdens and experiences with others, certainly within a school – and ideally across a number of schools – will help to improve techniques and to lighten the load.

A possible format for a mark book

History Department

Name:

Form:

Skills/Concepts/Ideas

Reference & information-finding skills	Skills in chronology	Language & historical ideas	Use & analysis of evidence	Empathetic understanding	Asking historical questions	Synthesis & communication

Level of performance

Stage 1																					
Stage 2																					
Stage 3																					
Stage 4																					
Stage 5																					

Table 3
Some techniques of assessment to measure objectives based on the practice in schools in one LEA.

Skills in Chronology

Skill	Suggested means of assessment and teaching strategies
Know terms: BC, AD, century, decade, generation	Provide dates in wide range, AD and BC: Pupil to locate in correct century Provide wide range of centuriis: pupil to give dates in first, last decade, half-century Generation: ' "I was born in 1970 when the nation was at peace. My father was born at the height of the Blitz in 1940 when my grandfather had just returned from Dunkirk". Around which date was my grandfather's generation likely to have been born?'
Sequencing dates	Match out-of-order dates with out-of-order events Arrange is order of time
Sequencing periods	Random sequence of period titles: place in order Match significant characteristics of specific historical periods to their period labels, eg Crusades, Renaissance, Edwardian, and to time sequence
Sequencing visual/artefact evidence	Provide evidence: pupil to place in time sequence and support choice with reasons Observation and ordering exercise eg in built environment
Time chart with scale comparative correlated qualitative	Arrange dates and events on a time line according to scale Arrange data from two different contemporary civilisations/sequences Arrange data to show interrelationship of different aspects, eg political, economic, technological Indicate in a time sequence strength/weakness of historical movement in graph form, eg Protestantism in Tudor England; progress in medicine

Language and historical ideas

Specialist terminology will need to be noted beforehand; a wide range of concrete examples or analogies will need to be offered to help pupils reach a definition in their own minds; provide structured tests in which terms are matched to examples, questions, or both, which require terms to be explained in the course of their answers.

Use and analysis of evidence[1]

Skill	Suggested means of assessment and teaching strategies
Understand role of evidence	Pupil to indicate types of evidence the historian uses; provide a simple definition. 'Give some reasons why the work of the historian is like that of the detective. The following words may be useful: clue, proof, evidence, witness, documents, archeology, finds'
Assess main features of concrete evidence	Provide simple artfacts, visual or environmental evidence: What is it? What was it used for? Who made it and why? Did it make any difference? Mark Pullen exercise: Schools Council 13–16 Project *What is History?*
Distinguish between primary and secondary evidence; understand their relative values	Provide a number of pieces of primary and secondary evidence for same event/topic: which are directly observed/related/contemporary; which are not? 'Clues, Clues, Clues' exercise: Schools Council 8–13 Project *Place, Time and Society* Provide primary and secondary evidence *both* of which show insights/balance and partiality/lack of balance. Pupils asked to compare and comment

[1]Grade according to agreed descriptions or criteria of performance, in particular the way in which answers relate conclusions to evidence; indicate gaps or inconsistencies; make simple generalisations using evidence; make reasonable extensions from evidence.

Table 3

Use and analysis of evidence Skill continued	Suggested means of assessment and teaching strategies
Statistical and diagrammatic evidence	Provide statistical data: pupil to arrange in graph or bar chart form Provide statistical, diagrammatic or map data: pupil to extract key points
Reconstruct narrative from different sources; compare different accounts of the same event, noting contrasts, similarities, gaps; draw inferences and construct theories in explanation	Provide range of sources (eg documentary, visual, statistical, oral) on same event/problem: pupil to reconstruct what happened; compare strengths and weaknesses of pieces of evidence; note similarities, contradictions and gaps Pupil (using same range of resources) to use the evidence to explain why the event/problem took place and developed as it did; offer alternative explanations and show how they are supported by the evidence; indicate what other information would be needed to offer a balanced explanation
Solve problems, reach reasoned explanations exploring alternatives	Eg Schools Council 13–16 *What is History?:* Tollund Man; Mystery of the Empty Grave; Princes in the Tower
Distinguish fact and opinion; partiality; bias; propaganda	Fact and opinion; provide contrasting sources, eg on trial and execution of Charles I: pupil to distinguish elements that can be cross-checked and those that come from author's beliefs or feelings Partial: compare sources that see only part of whole (eg battles, sieges): distinguish inadequacies and inconsistencies Bias: pupil to distinguish bias in sources known to have been gathered for a purpose eg visitation of the monasteries; 'Olympische Spiele 1936' Propaganda: pupil to distinguish deliberate distortions, eg in Nazi speeches; USSR and First World War posters

Asking historical questions
Skill

Be aware of basic historical questions: What happened and when? Why did it happen? How do we know?	Provide an account based on evidence: assessment by structured essay that requires pupil to indicate what happened, offer reasons for it and indicate basis of our knowledge Oral: tell story of sequence of events; identify pupils whose contribution is to be assessed; note main features of responses expected; check off features mentioned by individual pupils
Be used to asking questions about the main features of everyday life in any historical period: When and how did people live, feed and clothe themselves? What was the available technology? The life styles of different social groups? What differences between then and now?	Use reconstuction of the past eg living museum, Iron Age Village (TV): pupil to create an observation schedule and complete it Follow-up: project on social life of an alternative civilisation/period.

Table 3

Questions of increasing difficulty: Who governed, how, with what results? What did they worship? What values did they live by? What was their art, music and literature?	Picture interpretation, eg provide contemporary illustration of Elizabeth I in procession with courtiers: pupil to assess what sort of person has power, why processions of this sort held and why pictures of them? (Could be compared with photograph of Lenin's government after 1917 Revolution)
	Medieval illustrations of heaven and hell: pupil to indicate the preoccupations of the people of the Middle Ages from this evidence
Begin to analyse historical events by asking: What was the immediate cause? Did any long-term cause operate? Were there political, economic or religious causes? To what extent were personalities important?	Problem solving: eg Suffragette Derby 1913. Provide primary/secondary sources and a general account of suffragette campaigning; why did the Suffragette Derby happen? Assess responses in providing an explanation of underlying factors and the nature of the campaign, the choice of the Derby and the King's horse, the role of individuals and state of mind of Emily Davison, the effects of the incident

Synthesis and communication using basic historical concepts

Describe orally or in writing past events or situations recognising SIMILARITIES/DIFFERENCES with today, supporting account or conclusion with evidence	Provide documentary/visual evidence, eg Victorian working class life: pupil to identify similarities to and differences from today
	Provide documentary/visual evidence, eg life of farmworker in eighteenth-century England and eighteenth-century Russia: pupil to identify similarities and differences. Grade according to range of depth of comparisons drawn and use of evidence to support conclusions
Put together orally or in writing a narrative of past events or situations showing evidence of CONTINUITY/CHANGE and simple CAUSATION	Provide documentary evidence, eg of sewerage system of ancient Rome, industrial Manchester 1830, late Victorian London: pupil to identify main elements of continuity and change
	Provide documentary and statistical evidence, eg of supply and demand for thread and cloth in eighteenth-century textile industry: pupil to relate this to technological improvements
Write an explanation of a past event or situation in terms of CAUSE and EFFECT, supported by evidence	Provide a general account and primary and secondary sources, eg on Cortes and conquest of Mexico: Pupil to analyse reason for Cortes' success and its effect on the Aztec Empire
	Provide the defined causes/results of an event or situation: pupil to rank them in order of importance supporting choice by evidence.
	Grade for weighting given to particular cause/effects in reaching a credible explanation and for use of supporting evidence.
	Include irrelevant elements: Do pupils identify and reject them and give their reasons?
Write a clearly structured analysis, using evidence, which argues clearly to a credible conclusion; write an analytical account which takes into consideration different interpretations	Prepared answer essay: two problems set beforehand with evidence provided; agreed number of words on each prepared outline; the problem to be tackled chosen by lot at the beginning of the time allowed. Grade for: organisation of material; development of argument and marshalling of evidence; assessment of status of evidence; clarity and validity of general state and conclusions in relation to evidence
	Provide primary, secondary and statistical evidence, eg on Peasant's Revolt: pupil to determine whether a mass movement or an engineered rebellion. Grade for acknowledgement given to different interpretations and use of evidence; validity of conclusions in relation to evidence

Table 3

Empathetic understanding *Skill*	*Suggested means of assessment and teaching strategies*
Simple imaginative reconstruction of a situation in the past and how it appeared to some of the people in it, using evidence to draw, model, dramatise, write or tell the story	Life in sixteenth-century merchant's house: provide clear primary and secondary evidence: pupil to identify different parts of the house and their function; translate into a drawing or plan; describe orally, in role play or writing, the way of life of identifiable members of the household consistent with the evidence
Imaginative reconstruction, which is not inconsistent, of a past situation based on several pieces of evidence, including historical fiction, and exploring some of the feelings participants might have had	Provide three or four accounts from primary and secondary sources including historical fiction, of event or situation: pupil to talk, role-play or write about a specified participant's view of the event and the participant's likely feelings and responses at the time, eg. extracts from Tacitus on Roman conquest of Britain, Rosemary Sutcliffe: pupil to write an imaginative reconstuction of an attack
Can show understanding of a person's viewpoint within a historical situation; can consider the viewpoints of opposing sides and of people for whom they may not feel sympathy	Provide accounts from primary and secondary sources, eg Viking invasions, Saxon monks and Viking sagas: pupils to indicate in drama or writing the attitudes of each side: *or* executions of Reign of Terror: pupil to explore feelings of a victim; to argue the case for and against the Reign of Terror
Can identify the extent of choice available to a person in a given situation in the past; can identify the values and attitudes on which human actions have been based in the past	Provide primary and secondary evidence, eg William I and Harold: pupil to indicate, orally or in writing, the options open to both at particular stages in the campaign Simulation exercise: ironmaster: location of a seventeenth-century iron works in relation to raw materials, labour, transport, markets Computer programs, eg Francis Drake: pupil to select options, program compares pupil choice to Drake's actual choice

What was the disgraceful treatment of Joan of Arc?
What were the dying feelings of the monster Henry VIII?
Abridge the history of Perkin Warbeck.
Who was Oliver Cromwell?
What Kings were succeeded by their brothers?
(James Adair. From Five Hundred Questions Deducted from Goldsmith's History of England Calculated to Instruct Young Persons in the Causes, Consequences and Particulars of Events in English History, 1811)

The two illustrations give very different impressions of how farm workers lived in the nineteenth century. Does this mean that one of the illustrations is useless as historical evidence or could both be useful?

'Ireland is bedevilled by the problem of insecure minorities'.
Using precise historical evidence to support your point of view explain why:
i) The Catholic minority in Ulster has found it difficult to accept the political and social system there;
ii) The Protestants of Ulster have been so determined not to become a Protestant minority in a united Ireland.

(Two questions set in CSE examinations in the 1980s)

It is not just wider horizons and an increasing intellectual confidence and emotional maturity that distinguishes the 14 to 16 age group. For the first time for most pupils, the decision to study history is the result of a choice. Of course, that choice is often conditioned by option patterns, or by the difficulties of other subjects. Nor are all pupils necessarily, or likely to be, aware of the implications of their decision. Nevertheless, many do choose to continue their studies of history influenced by good teaching and by an enthusiasm for the subject. But, whatever the explanation, for the vast majority of these pupils, history will be studied as part of an external examination syllabus whose outcome will be seen by them, and their parents, as contributing to their job and higher education prospects.

The HMI survey of secondary schools,[1] commented on the effect of external examination syllabuses on teaching and learning methods. While it was recognised that they were an important element in motivating pupils and teachers, the report says that examinations 'affect the structure, content, and teaching of the curriculum and, in consequence, the atmosphere of the whole school'. There is evidence that 'a minority of schools go further and attach little importance to anything else'; '. . . in other schools rewards for endeavour were seen by teachers or pupils only in terms of certificates: in the process they lacked opportunity to explore the intrinsic interest of the subjects being studied'. The report added that '. . . some pupils responded by showing little interest in anything which was not seen to be related to the examination work'.

13 Nat Love – Source material from CSE paper

[1]*Aspects of secondary education: a survey by HM Inspectors of Schools.* HMSO, 1979.

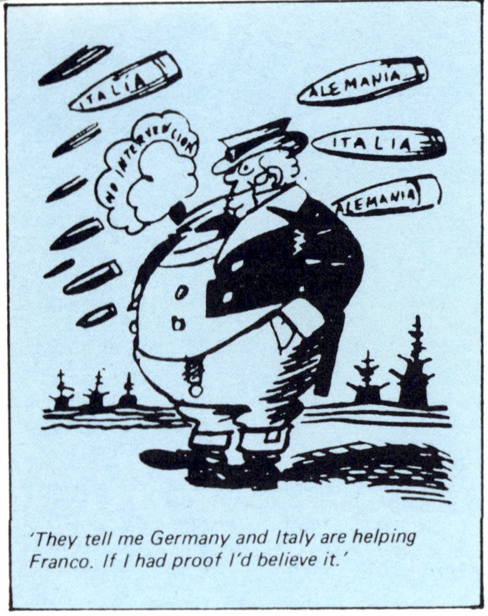

'They tell me Germany and Italy are helping Franco. If I had proof I'd believe it.'

14 Spanish Republican cartoon – Source material from O-level paper

Unfortunately there seems little doubt that many schools find it difficult to reconcile the demands of examination syllabuses with history teaching that extends and encourages more purposeful and enterprising reading, and gives opportunities for pupils to work independently on apsects of the past that have excited them. Nor do they often find ways of encouraging oracy sufficiently – discussing, listening, asking questions, and defending a case. It is these abilities on which much of the personal confidence and social competence of young adults depend. However, it is encouraging that a tradition of teaching that often emphasises too exclusively repetitive memorising and limits opportunities for reading and oral skills is being viewed increasingly critically by teachers and examination boards. Some examination syllabuses, including those based on the Schools Council 13–16 History Project and others examined under Mode 3, are showing that, within the context of external examinations, more enterprising and demanding syllabuses can be established. They show that pupils, not necessarily of the highest ability, can demonstrate a wide range of cognitive skills and an understanding of fundamental historical ideas.

Recent developments

Much work has been done in recent years to develop the national criteria for new examinations at 16-plus. Future syllabuses will define more precisely what is to be examined; grades are likely to relate to agreed criteria. Factual recall is likely to be less dominant. Pupils' learning could benefit from a more perceptive appreciation of how the approach to assessment used in some newer examinations might influence classroom practice.

The pressures for examination change are not only concerned with a statement of historical skills and concepts, but also with a growing conviction that the school curriculum as a whole should, by the age of 16, give pupils the knowledge and skills to support their understanding of contemporary society. For this reason, many schools are choosing syllabuses that have among their aims a placing of contemporary social, economic, political and technological issues in their historical context. By 14, pupils are beginning to understand and to question some issues in the contemporary world. For this reason, the case remains strong for keeping some element of history as part of the compulsory curriculum up to the age of 16. There are real problems of time and resources for some schools if history as a discrete subject were to be made compulsory for all pupils, although a minority of schools have succeeded in doing so. A few schools have maintained history as part of the common curriculum up to 16 by establishing it as an element in an interdisciplinary course (see Example 6, pages 54 and 55).

15 Surgery 1970 – Source material from CSE paper

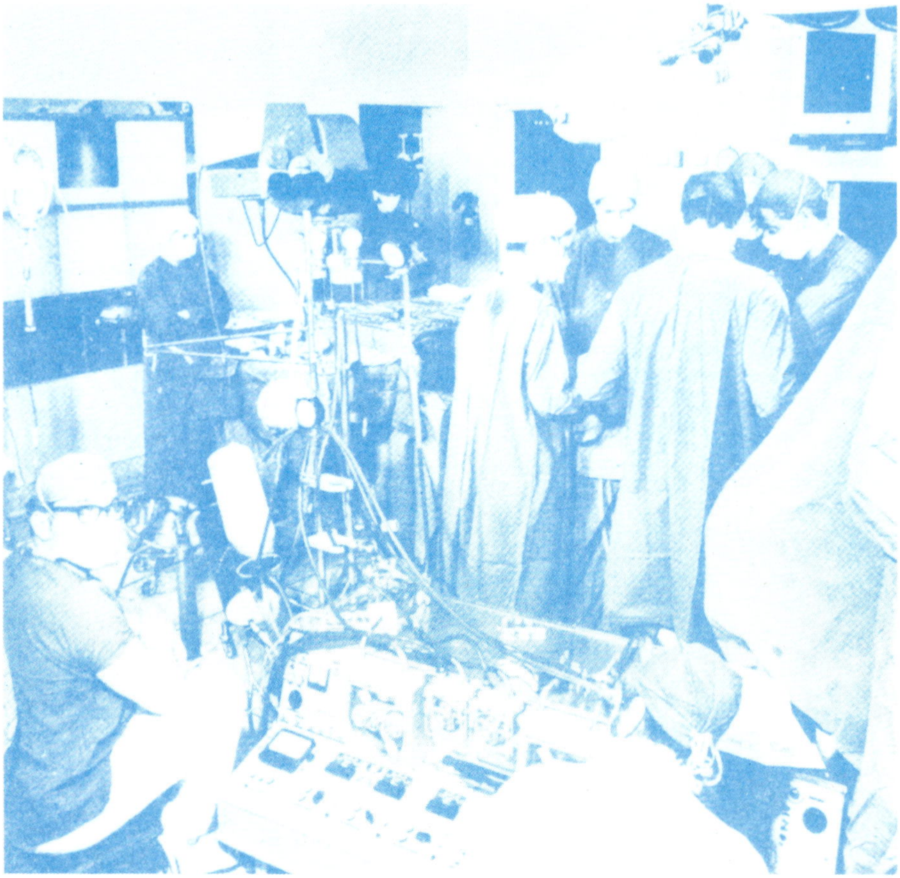

9 HISTORY AND CONTROVERSY

If historians accept that one of their roles is to put contemporary issues in their historical context, then attention will inevitably be given to topics that are controversial, even politically sensitive. Historians have on occasions been accused of either ducking these issues or teaching them unprofessionally. They have been urged to seek objective truth and content. But the inevitable selection, and rejection of content are value judgements, and the content of history curriculum can never be either objective or value free. However the *procedures* of history as they are described in this publication, are objective as they cannot be modified either by the ideas being examined or by the conclusions we may hope to reach. Thus they offer possible routes through sensitive areas so that professional and academic integrity may be preserved.

Three areas of particular concern are: sexism, history in a multicultural society; and bias, prejudice and indoctrination.

Women in history

Much written history has ignored women's lives altogether, or assumes that the history of men is the history of all people.
CAROL ADAMS

Just as it is important that a course of history should not give the impression to young people that British or Western society is either the only one or is necessarily an inherently superior form,

so too a course should avoid the impression that certain groups are inherently superior. This consideration might apply to small fractions of our society or to a whole sex. Increasing attention is now being paid to the way in which women perceive themselves and are perceived. However, the lack of emphasis given to women in history syllabuses may have helped certain popular stereotyped ideas to survive – that women have not been agents of change in history, for instance – and has had the effect of giving pupils the message that our society attaches low status to female concerns.

History syllabuses have tended to focus on women in three ways: the struggle for women's legal rights in recent British history, the women who quite exceptionally became military and political leaders, such as Boadicea and Elizabeth I, and women's work, usually manual work, in industry and households in the last two centuries. To restrict women's part in history to such topics is both to ignore and distort women's contributions to past societies.

It would be naive to expect evidence and its interpretation to suggest that women dominated political and military history. However, women have participated in government, reforms and revolutions on a wider scale than is usually indicated in syllabuses. Women have played a part as agents of change both within élite groups and as part of mass movements. In medieval Europe, Africa and India, women periodically took on responsibilities as rulers, regents, and military leaders; women

established Republican Clubs during the French Revolution and participated in the 1848 and 1871 uprisings. It was the Ladies' Land Leagues which for a period in the 1880s became the main focus of support for Irish tenants, and women industrial workers who began the strikes that led to the 1917 revolution in Petrograd.

16 Mary Seacole

Nevertheless the domestic, economic, medical and aesthetic spheres of human activity are those to which women have devoted most time and effort, and which have more significance in long-term rather than short-term changes. Yet in history lessons on the life of medieval peasants, for instance, it is common for an undue emphasis to be placed on men. In addition to caring for their families, women worked as blacksmiths, pedlars and shopkeepers, and took part in sowing, harvesting, slaughtering animals, fuel gathering, and defending their homes. In the history of more recent times, women workers are often shown to be passive, awaiting reforms, even though there are examples of women organising their own campaigns for better working conditions, such as the 'matchgirls' and Northern textile workers.

The domination of medical reforms by men in the last two centuries has clouded the much longer period when caring for the sick and developing knowledge in the use of medicines was largely in women's hands. Women have taken little part in some of the arts because they were excluded by the conventions of the day, but it would be wrong to give the impression that there were few women artists and authors in the past. Long before Jane Austen and Charlotte Bronte became established authors, women earned a living as writers. An example of this is the wave of women playwrights of the Restoration, some of whose work was still performed in Victorian times and is being rediscovered today.

Whatever their talents and inclinations, women's activities in many parts of the world have been limited by customs and laws. As well as being helped to understand the steps taken to achieve female emancipation (and not only in Britain), pupils could consider why restrictions were placed on women and why these restrictions endured for so long. Pupils could also think why evidence in history books gives little insight into women's lives. Teachers may find it interesting and useful to screen the materials they use in order to identify any implicit or explicit sexism. There are examples, in older textbooks in particular, of the use of language that assumes an inferior or demeaning role for females, and of reference to the physical appearance of female historical figures but not to the physical appearance of males. Similarly, there is often use of only evidence that renders women invisible or crucially dependent on men. The image created by this kind of material can be very enduring.

It is no longer acceptable to pay scant attention to women's lives in history. In the past, historians have been limited to their ability to write history giving due weight to women because of the lack of sources available, or because the lives of women were not considered significant. Recent research, oral history, and the reissuing of books written by women in the past have made accessible some of the sources needed to give a more balanced view of women's role in history.

There are, however, certain dangers:

• aspiring to reflect the changing views of our society can lead to the distortion of the past through special pleading;

• by shifting the emphasis from the study of elites to the study of the 'powerless', the major themes and developments may be lost and pupils can become bored and frustrated;

studying female roles as wives, mothers and daughters, even in an attempt at empirical analysis, can lead to the reinforcement of stereotypes;

over-simplification of the issues involved can lead to the study not of 'women' but of 'woman' – study that cannot be historical because it relies on generalisation and does not emphasise diversity and evidence. All of these dangers need to be countered in any attempt to challenge old assumptions about women in history.

History in multicultural society

More must be said about history in a multicultural society,[1] not only because it is an issue of considerable sensitivity, but also because much of existing practice seems to be based on unexamined, even conflicting, assumptions.

What *can* we say with any degree of confidence?

• Most ethnic minority communities in Britain are permanently settled here and the vast majority of the children and young people are British; they were born here and have no desire to live anywhere else.

• Educational aims are broadly the same for all children.

17 Buddha

Thus, education at all levels is concerned with British students and pupils some of whom are black, brown or white, are Muslim, Sikh, Christian or Hindu and whose family and community networks are confined to the towns or villages in which they live, or may stretch across countries and continents.

Added to those important statements is the fact that all pupils are growing up in a multicultural Britain. No history teacher can duck the question, 'In what way should the history syllabus in this school be different because my pupils live in a multicultural society?'. It is a question not only to be posed in Brixton, or Moss Side, or Handsworth, but also in Surbiton, Bodmin, and Norwich. It merely states, in a particular form, what has already been said – that a history syllabus must

[1] There is no generally accepted usage of the terms 'multi-ethnic', 'multiracial' and 'multicultural'. All have their disadvantages. Multicultural has been chosen because it attracts the fewest objections and its compromises are the least uncomfortable.

reflect key characteristics of the world in which young people live so that it can be put into its historical context. Ultimately, of course, the effectiveness of the history taught in a multicultural society will depend on its being supported by a school policy related to the entire curriculum. Some syllabuses that tackle this difficult question are still based on three assumptions that need to be re-examined. First, that any content reflecting a multicultural society should emphasise the recent post-war history of the Caribbean, the Indian subcontinent, or Africa. Second, that multicultural history is concerned principally with problems, conflict and exploitation. Third, that the teaching of those areas is *ipso facto* of interest to pupils whose families may have originated in those parts of the world, and that, for example, any black pupil will automatically identify with and be interested in the history of any black culture or individual. There is also the attitude associated with some of these assumptions – that the present generations in some way share a heritage of guilt for the mistakes, some of criminal proportions, of their predecessors. This point of view is neither morally nor historically justifiable.

In re-examining these assumptions and attitudes, four points might be borne in mind.

● The history of Britain as a multicultural society is a long one and is not just concerned with the post-war patterns of immigration from the Caribbean and the Indian sub-continent. The Romans, Angles and Saxons, Vikings and Normans have all contributed to our multicultural past. More recently, Jewish, Chinese, Polish, Hungarian, Ukrainian, Greek and Turkish communities have been established in many parts of the country. Internal movements within these islands of the Scots, Irish and Welsh also have origins, explanations and results that can be studied.

● An historical perspective also reminds us that the arrival and absorption of communities from outside and within these islands have not always meant, nor do they necessarily mean, tensions and problems. Frequently the mixture of cultures has been mutually advantageous, with significant economic, political, religious and cultural benefits. The exploitation, the unequal distribution of opportunities, and moments of tension and violence should not be ignored, but they must be put in a balanced historical perspective.

● The history of the arrival and assimilation of communities from overseas, particularly if they are studied in the locality or region in which they took place, demonstrates the diversity within groups which at first might appear to share common characteristics. In particular, pupils' pursuit of their own individual and family roots can be a genuinely historical and exciting enterprise. Stereotypes are challenged and modified. We can be reminded that Jamaica is not the same as Antigua, or the Punjab the same as Gujerat, that

history can help to identify the social and cultural differences that go part of the way to explain the existence of India and Pakistan and, more recently, of Bangladesh.

● Many communities are representatives of cultures that flourished with great distinction long before European colonisation. To ignore these achievements may serve to reinforce or leave unchallenged serious misunderstandings about communities within this country and may also lead to an unbalanced view of world history. A history syllabus, anxious to reflect a multicultural society, might well spend time looking at India before Clive or China before Marco Polo. The Crusades can remind us that at many points in our past Europe did not have a monopoly of cultural and scientific achievement. To such an approach, ethnic communities have much to contribute with their memories, beliefs, artefacts and culture.

However, such considerations of content do not in themselves dispose of other aspects of this problem. Multicultural history is frequently decked out with ambitious objectives, often not found associated with other parts of a history syllabus: to give minorities a sense of pride in their own group and cultural achievements, to reduce tensions and misunderstandings that emerge when different cultures coexist in the same society, to help individuals become more tolerant. At first sight it is difficult to challenge the worth of these aims. But they too are based on assumptions that demand re-examination. The first aim is based on an assumption that we *know* what gives any of us a pride on our culture, and that a largely white teaching force is able to give this pride to children whose family roots are in the Indian subcontinent or the Caribbean – an assumption which, if not innocent, is certainly patronising.

The second aim raises difficult pedagogical and political questions involved in teaching issues that are politically sensitive. There is a distinction to be made between such issues and those that are merely

18 Black servicemen in World War II

controversial; a controversial issue might be described as any issue that divides society or groups or individuals within the society. A politically sensitive issue, on the other hand, is one that may, or does, create a political problem for the school or a particular teacher or group of pupils within the school. It is the sort of issue that might arouse suspicion, anger or concern among parents, pupils, colleagues, or the local education committee. A teacher talking about Rastafarianism in the Brixton area might well be dealing with a politically sensitive issue. It would be no less controversial in the rural Home Counties but less politically sensitive. The pedagogical problems of teaching about the historical background of the Northern Irish situation are quite different in London than in Belfast, where certain aspects of the Reformation might be seen as more politically controversial than they would be in North Yorkshire. This is not meant to suggest that historians should avoid these issues. However, it may well be that the concepts and skills necessary to understand them are best defined and, so to speak rehearsed, in periods chronologically and geographically more distant.

For example, in an O-level class with many black pupils in an urban college of further education, black sensitivities to many white attitudes were a matter of great controversy. The white teacher rightly felt reluctant to tackle these issues directly, concerned as they were with a city where he and his students lived. However, an examination of race relations between white and black, the incidence of tolerance and discrimination, and the effects of emancipation exemplified by the history of the American South in the middle of the nineteenth century, defined certain ideas and introduced the pupils to skills so that later consideration of more immediately sensitive issues were easier. No general ground rules can be laid down. The particular circumstances of a school, indeed of a particular class, may well be the ultimate arbiter. Whatever strategies are adopted, they are likely to

be pursued effectively if they are related to modest and appropriate objectives. History teaching is not concerned with resolving this kind of problem nor is it directly concerned with the training for effective political and social action.

The belief that history can, in itself, eliminate prejudice either in society or in individuals is unrealistic. However, cautious objectives do not necessarily diminish the significance of their impact. Whatever decisions about content are taken, they will go for naught unless they are founded firmly on the skills of historical thinking with their insistence on the absolute necessity of having evidence to support statements made about those individuals or groups. Thus, correct historical thinking is the implacable enemy of unexamined and stridently asserted stereotypes. Historical skills may not open closed minds; they may plant a nagging grain of doubt in them. Historical skills alone will not eradicate prejudice or create universal toleration; related to appropriate content, they can at least make some considerable contribution towards giving tolerance an intellectual cutting edge to challenge prejudice. History, if not a sufficient, is certainly a necessary condition for helping young people to live with a degree of understanding in a multicultural society.

Bias, prejudice and indoctrination

The words 'bias', 'prejudice' and 'indoctrination' can become confused in everyday usage. Bias describes evidence that is selected or lacking in balance in that it artificially strengthens a case or weakens its opposition. Prejudice describes an emtional cast of mind producing opinions independent of evidence either by denying, ignoring or suppressing it. Prejudice frequently depends on unexamined stereotypes – for example, ethnic or sexual – on oversimplifications and careless thinking. Indoctrination is a process by which people attempt to persuade others to accept ideas and attitudes by suppressing evidence or teaching it so

selectively that it deliberately emphasises or conceals certain aspects. The link between the three words might be summed up by saying that indoctrination is the attempt to generate or perpetuate prejudice by the employment of biased evidence.

These considerations bear directly on the study of history in school. History can be an agent for indoctrination, but not as we have described it in this publication. History teaching will be a powerful weapon *against* indoctrination provided that it constantly insists on the necessary relationship between statements about people and available evidence.

But these approaches do not describe a value-free curriculum. A history scheme of work that seeks to detect and root out prejudice tries to examine all evidence so that young people have the skills and knowledge to choose between alternative interpretations or points of view; it also attempts to help pupils to understand the nature and origins of a pluralist society.

Prejudice can often lurk unintentionally and unsuspected in many textbooks and syllabuses – indeed, in the choice of words by teachers. It can lie in the unconsidered selective treatment of groups or countries – an image that, for example, suggests that Turks were principally concerned with invasion and massacres or that the Irish are of interest only when they are starving, emigrating or rebelling. But the very vocabulary history books employ can assume values that may betray prejudice: 'massacre', 'crusade', 'rebel', 'peasant', 'host community', 'civilisation', 'progress', 'bourgeoisie', 'discovery', 'imperialism'.[1] This is not to suggest that we should seek to avoid all such words, but to provide a reminder that the impact of words derives from their association and use as much as in their meaning, and that this impact can alter in differing social and historical circumstances. Recognising this fact is part of the task of detecting bias, evaluating evidence, and understanding the nature of historical language.

[1]See also 'Language and History' page 4.

10 LOWER ACHIEVING CHILDREN

Some pupils have particular learning difficulties that pose problems for history teachers and these have to be borne in mind if their aims are not to be threatened and their pupils under-challenged and sometimes patronised.

Six general points can be made:

● Many of the tools of diagnosis that commonly identify learning difficulties, or that measure, in the eyes of pupils, their achievements, are related to the skills of reading and writing. Books are read, many sources are written, communication is largely in exercise books, and the assessment of learning is predominantly in the form of written tests and examinations. Too many teachers are encouraged to pay inadequate attention to developing the skills of questioning, debate, the analysis of problems through discussion – in sum, to the skills of speech on which so much of the personal confidence and social competence of their pupils will depend.

● Many history teachers are now aware that language must be accessible and related to the understanding and experience of their pupils. The careful choice of books and the wording of school-produced resources is evidence of this. However, if the language is necessarily simplified, it does not follow that the intellectual tasks have correspondingly to be made easier. Indeed, making the language more accessible may create opportunities for increasing the level of intellectual demand.

● Many pupils, even by the time they have left school at 16, will not be explicitly using such ideas and concepts as 'chronology', 'change and development', 'toleration', and 'bias'. Nevertheless, the Bayeux Tapestry, for example, can be used to raise questions of bias; contemporary photographs of familiar sites compared with those taken a hundred years ago can illustrate change and development. In general, the more limited the academic ability of the pupil, the greater the number of examples needed to establish a given idea and the greater the need for opportunities for practical reinforcement before that idea or concept will be understood.

● Pupils' curiosity about historical matters may be developed if they are encouraged to use their powers of observation and enquiry. Fieldwork can involve looking at buildings, collecting pub and street names, comparing maps, charts and photographs, examining artefacts and museum objects, and assessing eye-witness accounts of events in history, which can be related to the memories of the recent past of adults they know. Visits to sites and other towns are also important, particularly if they are seen as integral parts of the course.

● Motivation is also affected by the limited attention span of some pupils. It may be that this problem can best be met by longer periods spent in well equipped rooms offering a variety of historical stimuli. Short periods, often associated with movement from room to room and adjustment from teacher to teacher, can disrupt the stability of a steadier routine based on longer periods of learning.

● Particular kinds of equipment will be necessary if pupils are to benefit fully from their history lessons. For example, tape recorders are a means of recording information and offering alternative roads to achievement for children who normally find writing difficult. One school describes the valuable support given to the history department by the 'synchrofax' or the 'talking page', and the 'language master'.[1] Both of these machines have often been seen as the prerogative of remedial departments, but in this school they have been seen as an essential part of assisting children with reading difficulties.

What schools can do

One comprehensive school in the North-East organised a course of 'remedial history' for slow learners and pupils with reading difficulties. Most of the work was concentrated in years 4 and 5 and was non-examined. The general framework for this course was broadly chronological, concentrating on the North-East and emphasising industrial and economic development. The main purpose was to strengthen basic skills by using them in history lessons and to develop new ones, particularly those of using and handling evidence:

[1]Hagerty, James, and Hill, Malcolm: History and less able children *Teaching History*, Number 30, June 1981.

LOWER ACHIEVING CHILDREN

- Although written work was encouraged, the emphasis was on quality rather than quantity. Hence, neat handwriting, well-presented work, clear graphs, maps, sketches, and so on, were encouraged rather than voluminous notes on given topics.

- Primary sources were employed, particularly maps and old prints.

- Trips into Newcastle-upon-Tyne and to the surrounding countryside took place and tape-slide sequences were produced. One particular theme emphasised the link between language and history and geography by studying place names and what they tell us about the past.

- Books were carefully selected so as to match the reading abilities of the pupils.

- Pupils were encouraged to reconstruct the past by various means. One of the most effective was the maintenance of the small history museum in the school. Pupils were encouraged to bring in objects such as miners' lamps and old 78-rpm records.

- There was a modest amount of model-making, mainly in order to develop manipulative skills and to give the children some idea of the basic working of machinery in the past – for example, George Stephenson's steam locomotive.

- Recall was tested in unusual ways. Assessment was frequently by oral testing and cast in the form of a game, for example, questions drawn out of a hat or box and fired randomly at the class.

- In another school in an impoverished inner urban area, a class of 14 year olds was studying war. The room was decorated with posters and photographs; it contained a pile of war-time local newspapers, a scrap book of Ministry of Food recipes, tin hats, gas masks, ration books, identity cards and call-up papers. There was a tape made by the school cook and by the teachers' charwoman recording their memories of air raids on the city. The narrative of the Second World War and an understanding of its impact on

19 Children using computers

ordinary people's lives was stimulated and enriched by a variety of primary source material. The pupils were being encouraged to collect, observe, and categorise, to consider problems of bias and authenticity, and to use their imaginations. The writing was marked for its imagination, its authenticity, its sense of period, and its ability to relate to what the pupils knew about trench warfare. Some of the more successful pieces of writing had been typed out and the spelling and punctuation corrected but the wording left unchanged: the association between writing and failure had been broken.

In one school where pupils were taught humanities, involving geography, English and history in mixed ability groups, units of material on local history had been drawn up with the advice of the remedial department on the suitability of language and the level of thinking. The teaching was strengthened by the presence in the classes of the remedial specialists working alongside the historians and their pupils.

In the first year of another 11 to 18 comprehensive school, 30 boys and girls of mixed ability were studying a course on the history and geography of Cheshire. To supplement extensive fieldwork, the department had prepared, at three levels of language demand, booklets of additional documentary and visual evidence together with open-ended questions

around which pupils could build their written responses. Essential historical ideas were common to all three booklets; only the levels of the language and the change from abstract to concrete examples were different. The oral contribution of pupils over the full range of ability indicated the interest and challenge generated by the exercise. For this approach, the department had used different strategies for different topics and these had appeared to meet the needs of pupils of a wide range of ability, including those who found learning difficult, while exploring the same historical ideas and skills on the basis of a common experience of fieldwork.

However, not all pupils underachieve because they have learning difficulties. Sometimes the most able may display learning problems because they have been insufficiently motivated and challenged by their history teaching. Much of the best work in schools demonstrates that, provided the language of history is accessible, the intellectual demands can be greater, and young pupils, for example, may well be able to use skills listed at the top end of Table 2. Developments within the GCSE at 16-plus are seeking to define much more explicitly and in some detail the necessary skills and understanding to achieve a particular examination grade. These grade criteria can also provide a practical working target for challenging the whole ability range of history pupils.

11 RESOURCES

What resources are needed to put into practice a scheme of work that will enable pupils to develop the skills and understand the functions of history? History teaching which aims to encourage independent learning and research and the opportunity to develop individual interests and enthusiasms, must enable pupils to use resources. This implies a fundamentally different relationship between learners and resources from that in classes where the teacher is the sole agent of their selection and use.

Space: The history room

In those schools in which pupils learn history as a separate subject – that is, in most secondary and in the top forms of many middle schools – it needs a base, a room with space and furniture that can be adapted to a variety of uses. In primary and many middle schools where history is taught as part of interdisciplinary or integrated studies, it is likely to be taught in a base shared with other areas of the curriculum. Whatever the organisation, rooms used for history need:

- to be as near to other history teaching rooms as possible;
- adaquate wall space on which to hang posters, project work, etc;
- blackout or, at least, dim-out;
- adequate storage space to house materials, permit easy retrieval, and include space for slides, film-strips, video-tapes and the teacher's reference material;

- book-shelves;
- map-rails and a globe;
- power points;
- a long working surface and a tracing table;
- flexible seating to allow group-work, debates or drama.

Books and libraries

Books remain the chief source of information as far as the historian's craft is concerned; restrictions on expenditure urge as effective use of them as possible. All pupils should be encouraged to use not only well-chosen textbooks but books with primary source material and illustrations of quality, books on single topics and individual lives and good historical fiction. Their work should encourage a confident familiarity with the library and all its sections, whether or not a departmental library is housed in the history room. If pupils are going to enjoy books and find them to be of service they must be encouraged to handle them with ease and confidence. This not only means acquiring skills of employing, as opposed to reading, them (using indexes, footnotes, bibliographies, etc); the books themselves must also be clearly catalogued, accessibly shelved, and available at times when pupils need to borrow, to consult, and to browse among them.

The following questions, addressed to the head of the history department,

reflect an ideal situation likely to exist in only a few schools. They raise issues that will affect the teaching of history and its management.

Access

- Is the library or book collecting reasonably close to the history room(s)?
- Is it available when it is needed?
- If you have a departmental library, have you established a clear working relationship between it and the school library?

Use

- Can pupils borrow books? If so, for how long? How are books recorded in and out?
- Are all the library books in the library itself or are some kept in the department?
- What system of classification is used? Do pupils understand it? Is a guide to classification prominently on display?
- Is there a clear and helpful author and subject catalogue? Do pupils know how to use it?
- Is the seating adequate? Is it convenient? Are there desks and tables for pupils to work at?
- Is there a system to make sure that books are put back in the proper place on the shelves?
- Are pupils given guidance on how to use the library's resources?

Content

- Does the library or book collection support the history syllabus?
- Are there books to cover the full range of age and ability?
- What skills do the history books develop or depend on?
- Do they direct pupils to other resources, including museums and collections of one kind or another, to be visited?
- Does the library also have collections of journals, maps and other illustrative materials?

Choice

- Does the library (school or departmental) make use of the county loan system, if there is one?
- Does the history department or the teacher responsible decide what goes into the history section?
- Does the history department influence what goes into the reference and other relevant sections (eg the social sciences and literature sections), bearing in mind that books of interest to historians are not only to be found in the history section?
- Is the rest of the department, or colleagues who also teach about the past, consulted when choosing books, or are decisions unilateral?
- In deciding between hardback and paperback, does the department take into account durability and permanence as well as cost?
- How many copies of a book are needed? What is the likely demand? Will the book be used by other departments?

Finance

- How large is the library allowance? Is it adequate?
- Does the librarian spend the bulk of the allowance early or late in the financial year?
- Does the librarian buy secondhand books and/or publishers' remainders?

Worksheets

Worksheets written by teachers require special mention as they are a popular means of directing and pacing pupils' work in some schools. They may be information sheets that contain primary or secondary material or both, or question sheets, or they may contain a combination of information and questions. For the most effective use, the purpose of the worksheets should be clear both to the teacher and the pupils. A worksheet may be the only way in which an unusual or relatively inaccessible primary document may be made available to pupils. Information sheets written at different levels of linguistic difficulty may enable pupils in one teaching group to gain understanding of the same topic. Questions that are both open ended, enabling all pupils to respond whatever their level of historical understanding, and structured, so that the intellectual demands of the questions overlap and build on each other, take time and care to compose and may usefully be presented to pupils on a worksheet. Where teachers work together as a team, mutual consideration of the linguistic and intellectual demands made of pupils by teacher-produced material will be of value to the teachers involved and will also enable that material to be used by members of the department with different groups. Presentation of all types of worksheet must be attractive, and it is essential that worksheets should be varied in format, in content and in the demands made on pupils.

However, worksheets are a controversial resource and generate strong opposition as well as support. Questions on worksheets sometimes require no more of pupils than comprehension of a simple text, and should more appropriately be written on the blackboard as the lesson proceeds. Presentation is frequently poor – smudged pictures or questions handwritten in haste. Variety is often lacking.

Teacher-produced worksheets and workbooks can be an important additional resource, supplementing and complementing books and audio-visual material. But lack of clarity in the purpose for which they will be used, lack of care in composition, poor presentation and over-use may cause them to hinder rather than develop pupils' historical understanding.

Source materials

Some teachers make effective use of collections of documents, artefacts, newspaper cuttings, maps, photographs and other ephemera. The nature of the collection will depend on teaching styles and the syllabus; clear and accessible cataloguing will enable it to be used to the maximum. Such collections can be usefully supported by photocopied articles, postcards, video-tapes, and audio-cassettes.

There is a wide variety of source material from which schools can draw – central government and local records, museums and LEA loan services, family and personal archives, archaeological sites, literature and art. Some may be in their original form, others facsimiles or photocopies, while others may be illustrated or collected within anthologies or textbooks. What form they take is less important than how they are used.

Audio-visual resources

Modern technology has extended the range of materials available to teachers and pupils so that, in addition to those excellent and cost-effective standbys, chalk and the blackboard, there are now overhead projectors, tapes, cassettes, TV off the air or recorded, films, film strips and slides. The BBC and IBA continue to offer diverse and distinguished support to learning history in primary and secondary schools in their television and radio programmes. Most teachers are very well aware of the range, and they choose from those on offer according to their judgement and the needs of the scheme of work. Some teachers are now realising the contribution computers can make to their teaching.

Is there easy access to:

- a record player
- a cassette/reel-to-reel tape recorder and a microphone
- a radio
- a TV set
- a video-tape machine
- a filmstrip projector
- a cine-projector
- an overhead projector
- a slide projector
- reprographic equipment
- hardware and software for computer-assisted learning (CAL)

Resources outside the school

The most accessible and often the least costly resource is the environment of the school. Some schools may be lucky in having a nearby parish church or a medieval castle, a Victorian or Edwardian town hall or railway station. Some teachers will heighten the observation of their pupils by encouraging them to look at pillar boxes, manhole covers, railings, brickwork, street lights, front doors, hedgerows, and field boundaries, clumps of trees, humps in the ground, and other unconsciously accepted but often unnoticed features of the environment. Some will have the more difficult, but by no means impossible task of devising lessons about the past from inter-war ribbon development, council estates and semi-detached suburbia.

All this work, and much within the school also, can benefit from the advice and the resources supplied by local services and public libraries and education officers attached to archives and museums. Many towns have local museums that illustrate the history of their own community and often have ethnographic collections from distant countries. A considerable number of national bodies are also able to give

advice and supply materials to support the teaching of history. Some, like the National Trust, the Department of the Environment and the Historic Buildings and Monuments Commission, are concerned mainly with the heritage of our buildings. Others give advice, and sometimes supply resources, about less accessible geographical areas – Europe, the United States, Africa and Asia.

Time

A history syllabus has to work within strict time limits laid down by school timetables; between the ages of 9 and 13, for example, most pupils have about 240 hours of history; in examination classes in secondary schools, the allocation is usually four periods of 35 minutes a week, and any less is unacceptable. History teaching that aims to develop skills and deepen understanding will undoubtedly be constrained by lack of time which will impose the need for a severely selective approach to content. Most teachers are likely to have little choice but to accept the given time allocation.

However, the distribution of time is also important. The variables that lie behind its distribution include the teacher's own styles of teaching, the age of the pupils, the type of work undertaken and possible links with other subjects. Double periods have certain pedagogical advantages. Longer unbroken stretches of time can be made more easily available if periods are timetabled consecutively with those of another subject whose objectives might have similar needs. For example, geography or social studies may also on occasions seek longer periods for simulation exercises or field trips, so that convenient interdepartmental arrangements can easily be made.

Fieldwork

Using the environment to support the work of younger children has a long tradition. For pupils in secondary schools, however, it has not always been

directly related to a scheme of work. Too often it has been a form of a peripheral treat at the end of the academic year, often supervised, and sometimes organised, by non-specialists. Fortunately, in recent years, there has been a significant increase in the amount of properly organised and effective fieldwork, often as the result of sensible collaboration between historians and geographers as in the Schools Council *Place, Time and Society 8–13* project or as a part of Mode 3 syllabuses or the 'History Around Us' unit in the Schools Council project *History 13–16*.

Fieldwork takes various forms: the exploration of a village or a town; archaeological studies (including industrial archaeology); visits to ancient monuments and sites, castles, churches and country houses; and related work in museums and record offices. At their best, such activities recognise and develop the interests and enthusiasms that many pupils bring to a study of the past. They can also develop in pupils a love and concern for the environment and contribute to the development of key historical skills. The potential of fieldwork is admirably summed up in some notes written for teachers engaged in the Schools Council 'History Around Us' unit: 'Specifically, it [fieldwork] gives children the opportunity to *identify, record* and *organise evidence for themselves*. A site is a quarry which they must mine for themselves; it is a source that has not been selected, edited, and paraphrased for them; they are brought to the *source*, but must understand and interpret *evidence* for themselves. Secondly, artefactual evidence is 'mute'; it purports to tell no story, and thereby presents several problems of evidence more starkly than is possible with documentary sources.'*

Computers

Almost every secondary school and many primary schools now possess at least one microcomputer. At the

---

*The Schools Council *History 13—16* project materials are published by Holmes McDougall.

present rate of technological progress and reduction in real costs, the use of computers in classrooms is likely to become commonplace within the next decade. Teachers of history cannot afford to ignore the computer and its associated software as teaching aids. Currently, there are too few programs and too little evidence of classroom experience available to gauge accurately how big the impact of computer assisted learning (CAL) will be on the way history is taught. At present, the computer seems to be most useful in two ways. The first makes possible simulations and games more elaborate than can conveniently be handled by other methods. The second provides pupils with ready access to large amounts of historical information and the facility to analyse this rapidly.

Computerised simulations can help pupils to use their historical imagination and develop their understanding of cause and effect in a particular historical context. One simulation, which could figure in the widely studied twentieth-century world history syllabus, makes possible a variety of different outcomes to the diplomatic negotiations over Palestine in 1947, depending on the policies and attitudes adopted by those involved. By repeated trial and much error pupils gain a greater appreciation of why the Middle East remains a battleground.

The facility to interrogate historical information such as census returns, parish registers, wills and inventories, makes it possible for pupils to receive a quick answer to a wide variety of questions, such as the relative size of professional and working-class Victorian families, the difference in the average age of death of men and women during the Industrial Revolution, and the disparity of wealth between landed gentry and small shopkeepers in the eighteenth century. Often these questions can be used to test, for one or more locality, the broad generalisations found in textbooks. Although the existence of a computer in the classroom does not guarantee successful learning, its use, either for simulation

or for information retrieval, encourages pupils to take the initiative to reflect, discuss and evaluate the evidence available, draw conclusions or make decisions.

Computer technology in schools is only just beginning to make its impact; other uses for it in history are bound to materialise. It can function as an electronic filing system for historical resources or as an aid to pupil assessment. When linked to video discs, it provides an instant display in diagrammatic or cartological form of

historical information far more extensive than in any existing map, history or historical atlas. Such developments would liven up the study of history for pupils of all abilities, not least those pupils who have learning difficulties. The BBC Domesday Project is an interesting example of a nationwide database compiled by pupils for future historians and using computers and video discs.

The rise of the 'teenage computer millionaires', selling their arcade games to software distributors, indicates how quickly the present generation of pupils has realised and exploited one potential of the computer. This is just an aspect of the rapid and far-reaching social and economic changes brought about by the computer revolution, the history of which is something that both professional and school historians will very soon need to study. In short, the computer is not just a powerful new tool for the history teacher; it is rapidly becoming part of history itself.

20a Early nineteenth century map

20b Aerial view of Tower Hamlets

12 CONCLUSION

History in the primary and secondary years seeks to identify the particular preoccupations and procedures of history, and to suggest some ways in which they might be made part of the curriculum for children between the ages of 5 and 16. It helps to identify skills, and how they might be progressively developed and assessed. It offers some criteria for selecting content and suggests that it be placed within some overall framework of historical knowledge and chronology. If pupils' understanding of the past is to be coherent and systematic it will depend on a far greater degree of consultation and cooperation between the different phases of education. This publication can contribute to that process.

The case for history

In February 1984 the Secretary of State declared his belief that history should be part of the curriculum of all pupils up to the age of 16. But options will continue to be offered to young people between the ages of 14 and 16. Is it acceptable that pupils should be obliged to choose between, say, history, geography, and subjects which encourage some basic economic awareness? The question recognises that history is unlikely to find a place in the core curriculum 14 to 16 as a separate subject, defending itself from its own clearly defined well recognised corner and enjoying its traditional place on the timetable. The case for history depends on a recognition by history teachers of its place in the whole

21 "Question Time" BBC television

curriculum. In particular, history's contribution to the core curriculum 14 to 16 is likely to be as part of carefully planned and evaluated alliance with other subjects. Its effective contribution to such arrangements will depend on history teachers being particularly clear about the nature of their subject and its particular contribution to the curriculum. This publication therefore can serve as an agenda document in discussions between historians and the teachers of other subjects as they seek to establish interdisciplinary or modular courses which not only define the complementary relationships between the subjects but protects the integrity of them all.

But would it really matter if schools did not teach history? Would it really matter – and it is not quite the same question – if the school curriculum did not encourage pupils to think historically? R G Collingwood wrote:

'Knowing yourself means knowing what you can do; since nobody knows what he can do until he tries, the only clue to what man can do is what man has done. The value of history then is that it teaches us what man has done and thus what man is'. We might add that it thus offers us clues to what women and men might conceivably become. History is part of self-knowledge and the development of moral awareness. Thinking historically constantly demands the questions 'What is it like to be someone else?' and 'How do I know this is true?'. These questions are assertions of intellectual independence. They do not encourage deference nor always give comfort. They are not likely to be welcomed in a closed or authoritarian society. Thinking historically is not only one manifestation of an open society, it is also one of the guarantors of its continued existence.

Our individual memories distinguish us from each other just as they do the national, cultural, economic and gender groups to which we all belong. Thinking historically strengthens our knowledge and understanding of our memories and gives us procedures to evaluate and learn from them. These procedures may increase our knowledge and belief in certain shared values. Equally they may instill a sense of informed unease about ourselves and the societies in which we live. But without the evidence and an historical context our attitudes may cling to stereotypes and seek refuge in unreal aspirations. Thinking historically helps us to understand how we have been moulded by the past and to anticipate the future.

The late Professor Lawrence Stenhouse wrote:

> To act in an historical context is one way to act intelligently. To act in an historical context is to act with critical consciousness of history, not simply to be acted upon by tradition. An understanding of historical context does not yield predictive generalisations but it improves our estimate of situations and hence our judgement of possibilities thereby helping us to escape being surprised – in the sense of ambushed – by the future.*

Thinking historically not only enriches the understanding and development of school pupils but also of society at large.

* From 'To act in an historical context', an unpublished working memo by Professor Lawrence Stenhouse, December 1976, and quoted here by kind permission of Professor Jean Ruddock.

22 "East meets West" – Whitechapel High Street, 1981 (this part now demolished)

APPENDIX 1: PLANS AND STRATEGIES

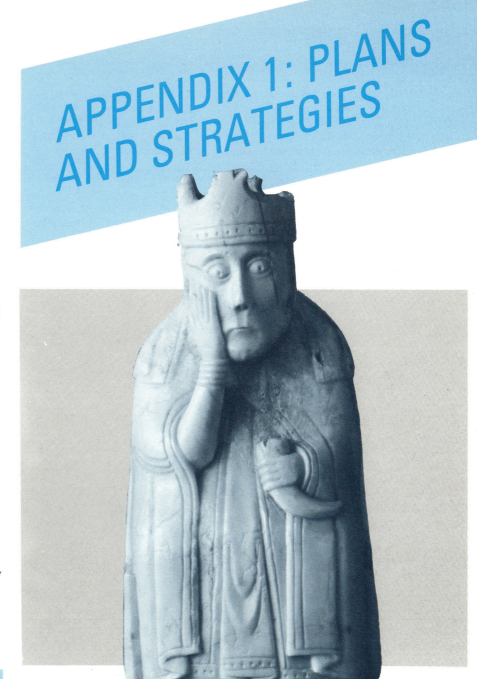

23 Lewis Chessman

This Appendix offers several plans or strategies as starting points for drawing up history syllabuses. Each is accompanied by a rationale explaining the thinking behind the plan. But they are not in themselves syllabuses or blueprints. They would need to be related to resources available in a school, to include the various skills listed on page 10, and to identify the particular assessment objectives and teaching methods appropriate to the school. They also need to be read in association with Table 2, pages 18 and 19. They can be adapted, or applied wholly or partly to age groups other than those described. They could well provide agenda items for departmental discussions and for meetings between schools or within associations of history teachers.

At the end of this Appendix there are descriptions of two Schools Council projects – *Place, Time and Society* and *History 13–16*.

Example 1
A primary school's approach

This example outlines the scheme of work in a 5 to 11 rural primary school and has been contributed by the headmaster:

Work of an historical nature has always been part of the teaching in our school. Until recently, however, there had not been any sustained attempt to give the syllabus coherence or structure. It was clear that provision in this subject area was uneven. Anyone taking an overview of the curriculum could discern a

certain aimlessness. It was not clear where work was leading or whence it had come. A written syllabus existed but it attempted to cover, or so it seemed, Western civilisation from the flints to the forties. Although this syllabus was generally ignored, its influence could still be felt and was one of the forces pulling the history syllabus towards a linear chronological approach. Within the school a variety of approaches coexisted uneasily. Some teachers favoured integrated work,

others preferred essentially undemanding schemes of work based on popular textbooks. The different approaches were not necessarily complementary and needless repetition did occur. Topic work in the best of classrooms was often historically weak. Lack of structure meant that children had an erratic diet which rarely helped them to get to grips with basic historical ideas or to facilitate their attempts to orientate themselves in time. All this was felt to be generally unsatisfactory.

The HMI primary survey[1] was published around the time the school came to review this area of the curriculum. This pointed up the inadequacies of which we were aware and led me, ultimately, to formulate a curriculum plan in some detail. The survey acted as 'a spur to prick the sides of our intent' but the time for curriculum change was ripe.

Eventually, this scheme was drawn up in response to a perception of the needs of the school. General principles and aims were first laid down and fundamental elements of the curriculum agreed. A concern with time, change and continuity, a sense of evidence of the past, and an awareness of the tentative nature of historical judgements were essential components of the scheme. We would also attempt to give children an insight into the complexity of human affairs and an awareness that man can influence events. The key role of books was identified together with the need to develop and extend particular itellectual skills, especially in relation to the written word. Inevitably, questions relating to methods, the allocation of curriculum time, record keeping, and resources were debated.

Having established a curriculum framework in terms of general principles, concepts and skills, the question of whether it was necessary to proceed to identify specific content had to be tackled. Some argued that to define content, even in broad terms, would be prescriptive and a constraint upon good primary teaching. Others saw content guidelines as liberating teachers from strategic considerations and enabling them to focus upon the needs of individual children and the problems of classroom management, as well as allowing for the efficient concentration of scarce resources. Eventually the scheme given here was adopted as an attempt to meet the needs of the school. It was intended to be a resource bank of suggestions from

[1] *Primary education in England: a survey by HM Inspectors of Schools.* HMSO, 1978.

which teaching selections could be made. Content guidelines, it was hoped, would make it easier to plan for the progressive development of skills and to achieve the general aims and specific objectives agreed. Leaving curriculum choice as a 'lucky dip' could involve unprofitable repetition and the omission of key ideas. Moreover, if the content of the history curriculum was regarded as important, it could not be left to chance. The history absorbed by the young child would, after all, form part of his or her personal cultural referents.

I am not arguing that a single best curriculum path for this school or for any school exists but that some paths offer potentially more profitable experiences than others. Some routes are foreclosed by constraints arising from the child's abilities or level of maturation. There are, for example, linguistic, conceptual and cognitive constraints upon approaching history as the academic historian does. But by whatever distance this school's scheme fails to achieve the optimum curriculum path, it does have the merit of being constructed rationally with the criteria for its selection made explicit.

The selection of topics was directed by the need to achieve general aims and made with a number of requirements in mind.

Content should be biased towards English history

This was derived from the general principle of working from 'where we are now'.

At least one perspective that is not national should be included

One major criticism of the undemanding kind of syllabuses I have already referred to is that they tend to be not only narrowly national in perspective but also nationalistic.

An attempt should be made to sample ancient, medieval and modern history.

Most primary history syllabuses (probably including this one) attempt to cover too much. This requirement was felt to be a useful rule of thumb.

Some history that can be personally related to the child should be included

This could be family or local history. Local studies might be balanced by the study of a distant place.

Unprofitable repetition should be avoided

This would give breadth to the curriculum and avoid the 'Romans and nothing but the Romans'.

The early secondary school syllabus should be considered

The primary and secondary school curriculum should neither be in conflict nor in ignorance of each other.

Fortuitous events that might give rise to valuable historical work should be utilised

The good teacher should not be discouraged from capitalising on the 'happy accident'.

The imperfections of this scheme soon became apparent and problems of implementation have had to be grappled with. But it was not conceived as a final solution, rather as part of the process of developing more effective teaching. In practice, when curriculum decisions have had to be taken in the classroom, it has often functioned as the arbiter of good sense, an impetus in a worthwhile direction.

The school's scheme of work

Focus	Notes	Suggestions, resources, etc.
Early Man	Blunsdon hill fort. Wiltshire ancient monuments.	Artefacts available from Museum Service. Use the hill fort. Possible visits should include Avebury, West Kennet, Devizes museum, and Stonehenge. Use sections of *Focus on History: Stone Age to Iron Age* and *Prehistoric and Roman Britain* by A. Jamieson. Wiltshire Museum Catalogue, pp 37, 58. Fiction: *Stig of the Dump* by C King
Ancient civilization (Greece or Egypt)	Point of comparison with primitive Britain.	Keep contact with the child's known world, eg use the Olympic Games or Pyramids as a starting point. Deal with specifics and avoid giving a general overview of ancient history. What was it like to build a pyramid? Why? The topic has to be highly visual (see filmstrip library). Note connection with RE. Make up hieroglyphics, retell Greek legends, etc. Filmstrips and notes on the Parthenon.
Personal history (or family)	The touchstone: something real and known to the children N.B. Opportunities to study pre-decimal money and non-metric measures.	The project might develop in a number of ways. Forget subject boundaries. A willing member of the family could be chosen, eg 'Grandma'. Important dates and personal dates can be compared. See *History not so Long Ago* and J Hagerty *Modern Britain*. Construct personal time lines for sequencing.
Norman Conquest	An invasion – the meeting of cultures. Change and the legacy of invasions should be examined.	A well-tried subject. The story of the invasion is an obvious starting point. Alternatively try taking the Saxon view through *Hereward the Wake*. Maps important; excellent scope for models and friezes. See filmstrip 'The Normans' (*History long ago*). Domesday extract available in Blunsdon. Try writing newspaper reports of the battle.
Medieval village (alternative focus: the town, the church, etc.):	Include a study of the local church.	Numerous books in the library. A time line showing the development of the local church could be made. Old maps (see village archive) provide details of ancient parish boundaries. Fiction could help to breathe reality into the topic, eg C Harnett's *The Woolpack* could be abridged for this age group. Consult *Round About and Long Ago* by E Colwell. Malmesbury Abbey could be an alternative focus.
The expanding European world.	Voyages of discovery: focus on individuals, eg Columbus, Vasco de Gama, Cabot, Magellan.	The Times *Atlas of world history* is an excellent starting point for teachers. The contribution of individuals can be examined. Narrative approach should be to the fore with opportunities for imaginative writing. 16-mm films are available and BBC history programmes are sometimes useful. See *Openings in history* 'Tudors and Stuarts', Sections 6 and 12.

A minimum of four topics to be completed in Year 1 and 2.

Focus	Notes	Suggestions, resources, etc.
Swindon and the GWR or The canal builders	Although there are many alternative case studies in industrialisation – eg factories, slavery – the resources for these topics are readily available.	Stress the human factor. Visits: GWR works, Kennet-Avon canal, Swindon town trail. Resources: taped interview with a retired worker; work-cards on both topics; old and new maps, eighteenth- and nineteenth-century maps. Excellent slides and filmstrips available. Museum Service catalogue, pp 50, 51. Useful sections in *Focus on history* – 'The Transport Revolution' and 'The Industrial Revolution' by R Unwin. Fiction: *The Butty Boy* by J Paton Walsh. Use time-lines, maps and sequencing games (see history games: resources).
Moving West (American history)	Aim to give historical substance to a topic frequently encountered on TV and in films.	A good opportunity to start with fiction: *The Little House on the Prairie* by Laura Ingalls Wilder, etc. The American Museum in Bath is an excellent source and worth a planned visit. Link with geography should be strong. Concentrate on empathetic response and relate to what they already know. Give essential time framework and context.

continued over

The school's scheme of work continued

Focus	Notes	Suggestions, resources, etc.
The Roman Empire	A non-national perspective. What is an empire?	Approach (as always) through the particular. The eruption of Vesuvius a good beginning. See *The Three Letters from Pliny* (CUP Classics Project). Map-work essential. Connect with biblical events. Note geographical work and the language possibilities. For Latin word work see *Oxford Junior English*, Bk. 5, pp. 18, 19, 40, 41, 46, 47. This project needs to be highly visual. Excellent slides, etc, can be obtained from a number of sources including the school library. Books: especially *Focus on History* – 'At the Time of the Roman Empire'. *Fiction: When the Drums Beat and Other Stories* by Geoffrey Trease: *Eagle of the Ninth* by Rosemary Sutcliffe.
English seventeenth-century history	To illustrate change across a period. Many options: social (plague, housing, etc), political (revolution, civil war, etc), scientific (Newton, Wren, Harvey), art (Shakespeare, Pepys, King James Bible, etc).	Do not attempt to cover everything; avoid overviews; stick to the specific. Opportunities for both field studies and individual work abound. See T Corfe *History in the Field*, pp. 125–128. Use 'Openings in History' (*Tudors and Stuarts* by D Kennedy) Museum catalogue, pp. 18, 19. Make up broadcasts, adverts, broadsheets. Fiction; P Lively *The Ghost of Thomas Kempe* and *The Driftway* (an account of Edgehill); C Marryat's *The Children of the New Forest*.
School journey study	'Distant place' – environmental approach. Use Blunsdon village trail for a comparison or an alternative if a field trip is not possible.	Field study centres and youth hostels can usually offer advice.
Saxon times 'Alfred the Great'	Story approach.	The use of imaginative story telling and visual material essential. Try starting with C Walter Hodges' *The Namesake* and *The Marsh King*. Note the local connection 'Alfred's Castle' and the battles on the Downs. Drama on the Downs is a possibility for the brave. Maps are again important as is a time-line. See filmstrip library and 'Saxon and Norman England' by H Pluckrose (*History All Around You*). Books: *The Way it Was* and *King Alfred, the Saxon leader* by J Blyth. Excellent maps and local information in *History Around Us*; 'Saxon and Norman Britain' by H Pluckrose. See Sections 17, 18, 19 of *Openings in History*; 'Saxon and Viking Britain' by P Wenham.

A minimum of five of these topics should be covered in years 3 and 4.

Example 2: A cross-primary and secondary approach emphasising local, national and world history for pupils aged 8 to 14

Example 2 consists of studies of local, national and world history over a wide time scale and includes ecnomomic, technological and social, as well as political, history. It represents a traditional strategy which emphasises, but by no means exclusively, British history. It is an approach which argues that children should understand the main landmarks of the history of the country in which most of them will live for the rest of their lives. The content is also broadly chronological but, to relate content to the developing levels of pupil interest and understanding, some topics are included out of sequence. The syllabus also attempts to give all pupils, before history becomes an optional subject, an introduction to the modern world.

The thinking behind the selection of content in each year described so that some appreciation may be gained of the difficulty, but also the necessity, of relating content selection to specified objectives in syllabus-making.

In the first year junior (J1) age range, stories are used as the main medium of learning because children respond

Local, national and world history over a wide time scale

J1
First year junior becoming 8

- A selection of myths and stories from the Ancient World, possibly on themes of creation myths, heroes and rulers (eg Nebuchadnezzar, Odysseus, Shi-Huang-ti, Darius, Alexander, Hannibal).

- Stories from British history, eg Alfred the Great, Robert the Bruce, Robin Hood (fact or fantasy?), Drake, the Gunpowder Plot, Pepys and the Fire of London, Nelson, George Stephenson, Florence Nightingale, Winston Churchill.

J2
Second year junior becoming 9

- A social history study.
- How we used to live 1900–1970

- A development study eg homes and housing through the ages.

J3
Third year junior becoming 10

- Stories of people and life in the Roman Empire, including Roman Britain.

- The invasion and settlement of Britain – Christian missionaries, Saxons, Vikings and Normans, including routes followed, great events and characters (eg Harold and William and conqueror), and the effects of landscape on new place names (eg '-ton' and '-by' endings, as in Northampton and Derby), and on language of new words from Scandinavia (husband, knife) and from Normans (pork, bacon, chair).

- The Middle Ages – medieval life in monasteries, castles and the manor.

J4
Fourth year junior becoming 11

- The Middle Ages (continued) – Henry II and his government; spread of Islam and the Crusaders; King John; Scotland, Wales and Edward I; rise of towns; the Black Death.

- Henry VIII and the break with Rome; Elizabeth and the Spanish Empire.

- Exploration of the world – Marco Polo and Asia; new navigational aids; Columbus and the exploration of America; Captain Cook and the South Seas; Livingstone and the exploration of Africa, including the slave trade; Scott, Shackleton, Amundsen and the Arctic and the Antarctic; Gagarin, Shepard, Glenn and space exploration.

S1
First year secondary becoming 12

- The English Revolutions – Charles I, Cromwell; the Glorious Revolution.

- The American Revolution.

- The making of nations – the French Revolution and the Napoleonic Empire and their effects on, for example, the Latin-American War of Independence and on Europe.

S2
Second year secondary becoming 13

- The Agricultural and Industrial Revolutions in Britain and their consequences into the twentieth century.

- The new powers in Europe – Germany and Italy and the First World War

- Empire to Commonwealth 1760 to 1960: stories of empire builders, emigrants and immigrants.

S3
Third year secondary becoming 14

- Changes in Britain since 1870 – industrial and technological changes; political changes and the Welfare State; immigrants and a multicultural society; changing status of women.

- New world powers – Russia and Japan.

- The Second World War; selected episodes to illustrate the aftermath of continued rivalry between the superpowers of the USA, the USSR and China (eg the Berlin Air Lift, the Korean War) and moves towards European unity.

enthusiastically to them at this age. This should not be taken to mean, however, that the use of pictures and artefacts is inappropriate. Myths and stories from different parts of the world, perhaps on themes such as 'creation myths' and 'heroes', will help children to begin to explore the distinction between fact and fantasy and give them opportunities to respond to narratives that involve values such as bravery, cruelty, loyalty or treachery. The other objectives behind the choice of stories are to enable children to hear some of the interesting tales from British history, from the past of the country in which they are living, so that they become aware of people whose names are part of folk memory or to whom national monuments, still to be seen today, have been erected – Nelson's Column, for example. They need not be told in chronological order, but whether they are or not, putting them in sequence on a time chart is essential if pupils are to develop a knowledge of chronology, and this itself is of value.

In second year junior (J2) age range, content is divided into broad termly topics. The first two topics are chosen to help children understand their immediate environment of locality, family and contemporary history. The development study if included as a specific attempt to help children understand ideas of change over a long chronological period, using a subject (homes and buildings) that they can easily comprehend.

In the third year (J3) age year, the first topic on the Roman Empire aims to introduce pupils to one of the great empires of the past that has had a major influence on Western civilisation and has left behind (not least in this country) a number of sites and artefacts to which pupils of this age can respond. Greek civilisation was not selected simply because it is more difficult to understand at this age and has left no tangible remains in this country. The second topic aims to continue the process of helping children to understand the history of their own country and, in some respect, the

continuities, between past and present. The third topic on the Middle Ages explores life in a different time.

In the fourth year (J4) age range, the first term's content aims to give some knowledge of selected people and events in the history of Britain, Europe and the Islamic world. The second topic introduces the break with Rome as an event so influential in the history of Britain and Europe that it cannot be ignored. It should be noted that the emphasis is not so much on the doctrinal Reformation as on the political break with Rome and its consequences for Britain, both domestically and in foreign policy. The work on Elizabethan England that follows links with this. The third term aims to give some knowledge of the ways in which Europe and other parts of the world were brought into relationships of varying kinds, both economically and politically.

In the first year secondary (S1) age range, the aim is to give pupils some knowledge of three major revolutions in history: the consequences of the English Revolution are still important in the political life of Britain today; a term's study of the American Revolution allows for some study in depth of an imprtant stage in one of the most powerful countries of the world; and the French Revolution had important consequences not only in Europe but elsewhere.

In the second and third years (S2 and S3) age range, the aim is to achieve some understanding of the modern world. The emphasis should be on the consequences of the events listed and the explanation of their influence on the present. For example, it is the continuing consequences of the Industrial Revolution for employment, trade unions and industry, the growth of cities, and leisure in the present that need explanation and not just the details of the first Industrial Revolution.

The syllabus as a whole has the disadvantage of allowing too little time for study in depth, though there is no reson why it should not be taught in such a way that the nature of history as

a study of evidence is pursued. It has the advantage of introducing children to a wide variety of historical experiences and of helping them to see that history explains the present, and the country and the world in which they live.

> **Example 3: An approach emphasising the nature of historical enquiry for pupils aged 8 to 14.**

Example 3 illustrates another approach to designing a syllabus or a scheme of work. Like Example 2, it is neither a rigid framework nor a prescriptive system. It can be adapted to suit the interests of teachers, the abilities of their pupils, the location of their schools and the resources available.

The principle of Example 3 is to introduce children to the nature of historical enquiry. Its starting point, therefore, is historical skills, or process; and, in particular, the use of different kinds of historical sources, the interpretation and understanding of sources, deduction, and the communication of conclusions based on evidence. Progression has been built into this introduction to historical inquiry so that pupils who have begun to learn history in this way in their junior years will be able to build on their experience and understanding when they reach secondary level.

In all years from first-year juniors (J1) to third-year secondary (S3), pupils should have access to, and their work should be based on, a variety of historical sources. As long as pupils are not introduced to exactly the same examples, their learning can be based on the same *kind* of sources in every year. Those that can be introduced to pupils are listed in an abbreviated form in the column headed 'Process'. Some kinds of written records are not necessarily appropriate to all pupils, but pictures, artefacts, the memories of people still alive, and sites are accessible to pupils of all ages and abilities.

Development in pupils' understanding of the process of historical enquiry comes in two ways: in the greater difficulty of the material presented to pupils and in increasing the demands that may be made of pupils as they gain in understanding. Two kinds of skills that pupils should develop during their study of history are listed: those described as 'history-specific' and those described as 'general' skills. Skills specific to history are those that pupils develop as they learn to handle historical sources: they are implicit in historical enquiry. Both kinds of skill are cumulative. However, to make the grid simpler, they have not been included for every year; it is, however, axiomatic to a scheme of work of this kind that skills developed in S1 are subsumed under S2 and S3. Therefore, it must be emphasised that skills acquired by younger pupils should be consciously reinforced in succeeding years.

This framework also includes detailed suggestions for content for S1. It also shows how certain frequently taught periods might be used to illustrate particular ideas or concepts. Some possible topics that might be covered in years J1 to J4 and S2 and S3 are given. The sequence of topics covered in J1 to J4 and S1 to S3 should be in chronological sequence. A continuous chronological sequence from J1 to S3 might be possible but is not necessarily desirable. The key factor in using this framework is to ensure that the content chosen appropriately illustrates the process.

This is a complicated scheme of work and in many ways it departs from more familiar patterns. Its rationale can perhaps be made clearer by detailed comments on one year of this scheme – for the 11 to 12 age group.

Concepts and ideas

During S1, pupils' concepts of *cause* and of *change* (both short- and long-term change) are to be reinforced and extended through the notion that societies changed from primitive hunter-gatherer forms, through agricultural slave-owning phases to early feudalism, but that such changes did not occur everywhere or at

unvarying rates. Other ideas, such as authority, technology, religious faith or industry, could be introduced at appropriate points, although not invariably by name.

The first year of secondary education is an appropriate point at which to help pupils understand that historical change is not an epic of 'progress', but that many setbacks, both natural and man-made, have occurred in our social and economic development. The content chosen by teachers should exemplify this. It should also reinforce pupils' understanding of the fact that past events were not one-sided. An 11 year old is well able to comprehend the different perceptions of, for example, the battle of Salamis held by the Greeks on the one hand and by the Persians on the other.

Content

Early people. Pupils are introduced to anthropological and archaeological source material regarding our ancestors, to wall paintings, implements, and so on, and to what they tell us about the art, beliefs, technology and organisation of societies 15,000 or more years ago. It is important to emphasise the significance and magnitude of inventions such as metallurgy or the sowing of crops, and to illustrate the change from hunting and gathering to agriculture.

Egypt and the Middle East. A great many archaeological sources – pictures, hieroglyphs, and artefacts from tombs, for example – can be used effectively in history classes. There is the testimony of buildings – in particular, the pyramids – and what they can tell us. What they do not tell us – how they were built – has still to be worked out. They are part of the evidence about the organisation and assumptions of the Egyptians; their religion; their art (tomb furniture, and so on); their technology, especially irrigation and hydraulics; and their knowledge of mathematics and astronomy. The story of the Rossetta stone is another example of historical detective work. The sheer duration of the long dynasties will in

itself be a helpful addition to the chronological map being built up by the history course. Thus, this section of content should develop the evaluation of different kinds of sources, and it can offer useful practice in graphics, number and skills of craft, design and technology.

China is studied as an important contrast, different from the more familiar Western sources of secondary history, but the origin of many things we take for granted. These are examples of great technical achievements (the building of the Great Wall) and artistic ones (the production of silk, glass and cast iron). This section aims to correct Eurocentric views of history, as well as to expose pupils to unusual and attractive primary sources.

Greece and Rome. This section poses the question whether the great classical legends are historical sources, and if so what do they show? Our own language, with many traces of Latin or Greek words, is another source (and one that can strengthen language skills in the course of study): Greek mathematics, notably geometry, can give pupils an exercise in 'historical reconstruction' as well as suggesting to them that Greek civilisation made exciting intellectual advances. This section could cover the main events of the classical world and suggest some of their long-term outcomes, eg Actium, the establishment of the Roman republic, the invasion of Britain, and societies based on slavery.

Britain. After half-term of the second term, the course can move towards British history by linking it with the Greeks and the Romans, and by summarising some of the previous work. The achievements of the builders, of Stonehenge and of the villas and roads of Roman Britain, could stimulate possible fieldwork. Other topics are the *Völkerwanderung* and waves of early immigrant peoples, such as the Celts, with the traces of their language and artistic achievements, and the eruption of the Vikings – an example of man-made disasters striking settled communities (although this

An emphasis on historical enquiry

Content: Possible topics – A few examples	General Skills	Historic-specific skills	Process
J1 Family history: concentrating on life two generations ago	**Language:** Listening, pupils describing in their own words in speech and in writing. **Graphical:** drawing or painting from observation reference: eg the use of page numbers. **Number:** scale and measurement	Children's skill in asking questions of evidence Learning historical sequence, eg 'now', 'not long ago', 'generation'	Oral evidence. Photographs, portraits, statues Sites Artefacts
J2 Life in a manor, castle, or monastery. Famous people of the time: eg Chaucer, Thomas à Becket, Bede, Richard I, Wat Tyler or, as in Eileen Power's *Medieval people*, Bodo the Peasant, the Pastons	As above **Language:** oral: forming hypotheses	As above, but the capacity to ask questions is to be reinforced, eg **How do we know? What happend and when? Why did it happen? What was it like then?** Awareness of contrasting evidence Historical language and **terminology: eg true/untrue king/queen/nobles**	Photographs and brasses Sites Buildings Artefacts Written evidence (primary): contemporary descriptions of famous people Written evidence secondary): about famous people
J3 Local history: immediate community county town or metoroplitan centre – nineteenth-century industrial conurbation	As above **Language** supporting statements with evidence in speech and writing **Reference** locating information, using indexes and audio-visual aids Translation of information into maps or diagrams	As above Understanding and converting primary evidence into a form different from the original Historical language: terminology, eg BC, AD; nomenclature of certain historical periods, eg medieval	Sites Buildings Written evidence (primary): eg census returns, directories, parish registers Original maps Place names and language derivation Secondary writing: guidebooks, writing based on primary lists
J4 Local history – Some national history – British imperial and colonial history – Multicultural history	As above **Language:** • constructing an historical narrative • pupils making their own notes from several sources Graphical number; accurate mapwork and diagrams, eg scaled time charts **Reference:** the use of a library catalogue	As above Assess the value of secondary writing and historical fiction	Pictures Sites Artefacts Written evidence (primary): Contemporary description of events. Written evidence (secondary): • about events examined through primary sources • historical fiction

An emphasis on historical enquiry continued

Content: Possible topics – A few examples	General Skills	Historic-specific skills	Process
S1 See pages 99–102 detailed suggestions for S1	As above **Language** grammar, the use of the appropriate tense and conditional mode **Notetaking** – an ability to categorise information into main and subpoints. Précis **Number:** the conversion of number values, distances and currency, accurate estimation **Graphical:** the ability to take photographs of sites and buildings, and to draw diagrams to scale **Recording** in alternative ways eg model-making	As above Induction, evaluation and weighing of different kinds of evidence: • comparing with like • comparing like with unlike • examining for bias • examining for deficiencies (the extent of the evaluation will depend on aptitude of the pupils) An introduction to dating techinques A comparison of secondary writers on the same topic	Pictures Buildings, artefacts, roads Legends contrasted with results of archaeology Written evidence (primary): • chronicles • letters • travellers' descriptions Primary/secondary: contemporary historians, eg Herodotus, Caesar Secondary evidence: • as a record of primary, eg aerial photographs • about primary, eg archaeologists' reports • textbooks
S2 'Patches' chosen from British history	As above **Language:** • precise written description and recording • the ability to argue a case orally and in writing • the use of a variety of sources in descriptive writing **Reference:** the ability to extract information independently from pictorial, archaeological and written sources	As above Inductive evaluation (as Year 1)	Pictures, including embroidery Archaeology Written evidence (primary): • poetry • legal – court cases • parliamentary debates • newspapers (secondary): as S1
S3 'Patches' from nineteenth – and twentieth – century European and world history	As above **Language:** essay writing – • as synthesis • as synthesis with examples • as synthesis with argument and thesis **Reference:** precise referencing of material, eg bibliographies, footnotes	As above The use of evidence by pupils: collation, conflation, cross-referencing, correlation Historical generalisations and judgements The interpretation and use of evidence in an attempt to develop explanations Historical controversy and comparison of secondary sources	Primary/secondary evidence: a film b novels, eg Solzhenitsyn Dramatic reconstruction in film or drama: a primary, ie written or edited at the time b secondary, ie written or edited later, strict or imaginative simulation. Historians' writings: comparison of a historians writing at the time b later historians c present-day historians

would not be the Viking point of view) – with further evidence from place-names, burial sites and the objects found on them, coins and sagas. Similarly, Anglo-Saxon England is being studied through its remains and writings. The prose style of, for example, Asser, Bede and the Anglo-Saxon Chronicle is concrete and accessible to pupils in this age range.

End of the year. Towards the end of the year's course, pupils can take stock, exercise their skills and look ahead. First, not all evidence is unambiguous. Did the Vikings reach America? Is the Vinland map real or bogus? The 'Bermuda Triangle' or suggestions that space travellers visited our planet in ancient times are good examples of

pseudo-mysteries created by historians who take advantage of weak historical skills in others. These could be taken as further examples and are probably very interesting for 11 year olds. Pupils might take stock in other ways: we are now at c1000 AD with about 27 million people in the world having achieved much since palaeolithic times (long-term change) but we are on the verge of other changes (in the shorter term) such as the Crusades and the Norman Conquest, or the clashes of cultures hitherto relatively separate (Islam, Christianity, China, the Mongols, and pre-Columbian America). Technology is moving rapidly into new areas: wind and water mills, clocks and great architecture. The year's work has moved from primitive, hunting

societies to early feudalism in the West, from knapped flints to T'ang ware. All these are examples of dramatic change.

Example 4 – an approach for the first three years of secondary school, taking London as its starting point

This syllabus, and its rationale, was written by Dr Richard Tames of School of Oriental and African Studies, University of London. It is included with his permission.

Example 4 is intended to be the framework for a three-year syllabus for pupils aged 11 to 16 years in London.

Example 4: A syllabus taking London as its starting point

A London	B The national dimension	C Linkages	D Comparisons
Roman London – Boadicea's revolt and the destruction of the city	Resistance to Roman *rule* British culture/Roman culture Processes of *change* (conquest, construction and conversion) The Roman Legacy	The Roman army St. Paul	Harappa or Ancient China
Chaucer's London – The Peasants' Revolt	*Kingship* and *Court* life The medieval village community – self-sufficiency and contacts with a larger world The *universal* church	*Pilgrimage* – to Rome, Spain and Jerusalem	Muslim Spain – court and city – Hajj
Pepys's London – The Great Fire	Old and New St. Paul's – *style* in architecture. People in portraits – Charles II and his friends – patronage and personality – science and music	Overseas *trade* – the East India Company	Mughal India (or Ottoman Turkey) – Taj Mahal (or Blue Mosque) – people in portraits – science and music
Revolution and Regency – The Gordon Riots	Riots and revolutions – Britain, France and America	*Colonisation* – sugar and slaves in the West Indies	West Africa and the West Indies
Victorian London – The Great Exhibition	*Living standards* and life-styles Railways and their impact *Charity* and *welfare*	*Migrants* from Britain	North America – settlers and railways
Inter-war London – The General Strike and the Jubilee	Motors and mass media Depression, democracy and dictatorship	1940	Allies and afterwards

The strategy of this scheme can, of course, apply to any large city. It can also provide an agenda for discussion between primary or middle schools and their secondary school to produce a coherent syllabus for the 9 to 14 age group. It aims to achieve a balance between local, national and world history, between the use of secondary and literary sources on the one hand and primary and physical sources on the other, and between dramatic events and significant personalities to stimulate the imagination. Finally, it aims to enrich the understanding with basic concepts and theories about human behaviour.

Selection of content

The rationale for content selection is as follows:

Column A – London
This is local history writ large, with London considered from two perspectives – as a community in its own right and as the national capital. In each instance, consideration would initially be given to the size of the city and its most significant landmarks and monuments, whether extant or not. In each instance, this is to be followed by a dramatic incident which can (in most cases) not only be related to first-hand sources, both visual and verbal, but also to matters of more than local significance.

Column B – The national dimension
The intention here is to take up in more general terms the specific issues raised by the dramatic events presented in A. Comparisons with other contemporary societies could obviously be made.

Column C – Linkages
The aim here is to consider a topic which has both national and global significance and which, therefore, can lead from the one to the other. There is ample scope for mapwork here.

Column D – Comparisons
The objective here would be to make, at least, *some* comparisons that would highlight basic points made under headings A, B or C.

Example 5: A multi cultural approach in a secondary school

This example shows the broad outlines of the history syllabus taught in a multiracial 11 to 18 boys' comprehensive school in South London. Certain major themes run throughout the whole syllabus: links between local, national and world history: the long history of Britain as a multicultural society: the fact that contact between cultures has a variety of causes and results, sometimes exploiting, sometimes beneficial; and the need to examine, with evidence and without prejudice, a variety of other cultures. Some of the details – in particular the details of resources – firmly fix the school in its locality. But its overall strategy and the particular themes with which the syllabus is concerned suggest a plan worthy of serious consideration by any school, whatever its geographical location or the cultural background of its pupils.

The head of history writes of this syllabus:
'Besides having the usual range of skills and concepts, the course aims to inform the student about the roots of many of the issues to be faced in the world and to make it clear that possibilities exist for change in the sense that human beings act on as well as react to the world. We are also aware of those distortions relating to culture and civilisation that are a negative legacy of Britain's imperial past. Part of the course is concerned with challenging assumptions and stereotypes about different parts of the world – what I once heard referred to as 'dispelling ignorance'.

'One important purpose is to pose the question "Who are the British?" as a challenge to the assumption often made that we are an Anglo-Saxon people. The course considers the cultural contributions of many settlers from the Celts onwards. In addition to the better-known groups, it features the experience of the Jews, the Huguenots and the Africans. It can operate on two levels. It deals with the complexity of the experience of those groups in Britain but also with the bare fact that Britain has been a multicultural, multifaith, multicoloured society for much longer than traditional wisdom accepts.

'We spend half a term each looking at major world societies in Europe, Africa, Indian, China, the Caribbean, and North and South America. We look briefly at how those areas changed between 1400 and 1900 through a consideration of the varieties of contact that were possible. Settlement is an important theme in American history and for Europeans in Africa. We complicate the issue by classifying non-whites as settlers in Britain, and can compare and contrast the Atlantic slave trade with British convict transportation.'

'Micro-history also features through an examination of Victorian education in Lambeth, the development of transport in South London, and a consideration of personalities linked with the area. These include Dr Johnson, who relaxed in Streatham, and his black servant and legatee, Francis Barber. Other black locals include the Shakespearian actor, Ira Aldridge; the composer, Samuel Coleridge-Taylor; and the Battersea Mayor and Pan-Africanist, J R Archer.'

'Finally, our orthodox twentieth-century history course also enables valuable insights to be made that contribute to a better understanding of the society we live in. Most pupils study the two World Wars; a portion of this time is spent looking at people from the West Indies and Africa, in particular, those who gave their lives or time for the "mother country". This is an unfashionable view for some. It is also an historical reality. We are certainly trying to debunk old myths, but, we hope, not at the expense of creating new ones.'

A multicultural approach

	Topics and concepts	Skills	Resources
Year 1	**Term 1:** Britain's long history as a multicultural society since 500 BC	Reference, map interpretation, story writing disciplined by historical facts, descriptive writing, appreciation of change and continuity.	School-produced booklets and worksheets on population movements; *Celts and Romans* (Macdonald).
	Term 2: Population movements; a contrasted society: Peru – historical and present day.	Mapwork related to physical geography, interpretation of visual evidence, continuity and change.	ILEA pack on 'Peru: the Quechua' includes worksheets, slides and tapes.
	Term 3: London and the local environment and their populations	As above (terms 1 and 2) related to local examples.	School-produced booklets: *London AD 61–160 The Plague, The Fire;* extracts from Mayhew contemporary maps; book: *Living in Lambeth;* local surveys.
Year 2	• The people who came to Britain: Vikings, Normans, Jews, Africans, Irish, Europeans. What are the British? Concepts: settlement, culture, identity, cultural contributions and survivals. • Local and social history: transport, education, leisure. Concepts: space, time locality, growth and development, past and present (similarity and difference).	Appreciation of visual and written evidence, bias; development of comprehension of primary and secondary sources. Awareness of anachronism and empathy and the recreational possibilities of London's heritage.	School-produced booklets, slides, Schools Council project materials, story telling. Interviews, museum objects, film. Visits to Tower of London, Museum of London, and London Transport Museum. *Immigrants to England* (Wayland), *Black settlers in Britain* (Heinemann), *Vikings, Normans* (Macdonald), *Detective work* (Schools Council 13–16 History Project).
Year 3	• The world in 1400: 7 areas – North America, South America (Incas), Europe, Africa, the Caribbean and China. Key ideas: that different cultural experiences are given equal and respectful consideration; parity of esteem of different cultures to counter racism. Concepts: social organisation, economic organisation, power relationships, influence of religious thought, beauty of material objects. Leading to study 'Contact': accounting for change in 7 areas from 1400 to 1900, independence to dependence without a Eurocentric/ethnocentric standpoint.	Appreciation and interpretation of evidence, speculation, application of general concepts. Recognition of complexity of historical explanation and lack of simplistic explanations. Development of appreciation of temporal and geographic factors.	School-produced booklets with documentary evidence, visual and audio material, films, visits to Museum of Mankind. Books, published and school-produced worksheets, films, videos, and slides. *People who came*, Books 1 and 2 (Longman), *Evidence: the Middle Ages* (Blackwell), *Toussaint L'Ouverture, James Cook RN, Pocahontas, Let My People Go* (Hutton), *Industrialisation: History Alive* (Blond).

A multicultural approach continued

	Topics and concepts	Skills	Resources
Year 3 *continued*	Relating the key concepts: cooperation, exploitation, rejection, settlement, mission, forced movement, refuge, resistance, voluntary movement.		
	● The twentieth century and the 7 areas: change, similarity and differences.	Development of speculation and formulation of hypotheses.	As above.
	● Industrialisation and imperialism: Britain's industrialisation and world domination to 1900. Concepts: progress, social change, production, surplus wealth, exploitation, automation, domination.	Further development of empathy. Ability to draw parallels with the present.	
Year 4 **O-level + CSE** **Mode III**	*Chronology of the twentieth century* World in 1900; World War I and impact; development of Communism in the USSR to 1953; Britain, France, rise of Fascism; USA – prosperity and depression; World War II; Cold War; development of Communism in China to 1949; the Commonwealth and independence movements. Concepts: continuity and change; Fascism, Communism, Socialism, liberal, capitalism; role of human beings in charge; evidence; bias, prejudice.	Development of narrative related to description, interpretation and imagination.	Course booklets; film and video. Discussion – use of Imperial War Museum. *Russia in revolution, Nazi Germany* (Heinemann); *Success in Twentieth-Century World Affairs* (Murray).
Year 5 **Examination** **courses** **continued**	Depth study of Nazi Germany at O-level, Italian Fascism *or* World War II. Course and conflict in Middle East *or* in Ireland. Consequence of Chinese Revolution *or* twentieth-century industrialisation. History of working people in Lambeth *or* history of the Black Experience or, at O-level, Southern Africa and Caribbean independence. Concepts: cause, conflict, change, identity.	Development of human sympathy, empathy and understanding: ability to cope with conflicting historical resources.	Continued use of class topic books, documentary evidence. *Rise of Communist China, Arab-Israeli conflict* (Schools Council 13–16 History Project); *Jamaica* (Oxfam).

Example 6: a combined course in a secondary school

In some schools, history is part of the common core for all pupils in Years 1 to 5, although this arrangement is comparatively rare. The subject may be offered in the form of history standing by itself, or it may be combined with other subjects in some kind of integrated or combined syllabus. Example 6 is to be found in a mixed comprehensive school of some 1,300 serving a rural and urban catchment area in the south of England. In this syllabus full advantage is taken of the possibilities of combining and cross-referencing the separate subjects; great care is nevertheless taken to ensure that the skills, concepts and content of history are in no way diminished in this combined course. Much depends on detailed and continuous planning and evaluation of all work to ensure that the collective specialisms of the humanities team are used appropriately and that the main aims of the course are being achieved. Among these aims are:

to encourage individualised learning;

to present information succinctly by oral, written and graphical means;

to handle a wide variety of forms of evidence;

to develop moral sensibility;

to develop skills in the specialist subjects that make up the humanities department (history, geography and social science).

The main features of the syllabus are outlined below. Subject and fields other than history are put in brackets.

Each of these topics makes it possible to interrelate history, geography, economics, politics and sociology. The role of history is important in each topic because of the subject's power to synthesise individual and detailed developments into a coherent whole and to explain some of the processes of change.

A combined course

Year 1

Unit 1 Change	An attempt to make pupils aware that society is always in a state of change; this unit also aims to familiarise pupils with methods of working in the humanities department.
Unit 2 Myths	How people make sense of their condition in different times and places. Particular reference is made to Greece, but also to Iceland, Egypt, Babylonia, China and Israel.
Unit 3 (Geography)	Reading maps. Different types of map.
Unit 4 Evidence and recording	A study of the ancient people of the county and their archaeological remains as evidence of life 3,000 years ago. Pupils are trained in evaluation and the recording of evidence.
Unit 5 Settlement and change	Roman Britain; a combination of history and geography. Causes of changing patterns of settlement.
Unit 6 (Geography)	Further map-reading skills.
Unit 7 (Geography)	Field study of a local village.
Unit 8 Evidence – variety and bias	The Norman Conquest and the Bayeux Tapestry. Students' experience of evidence is extended. Evidence is scrutinised for bias.

A combined course continued

Year 2

Unit 9 Patch and evidence	Life in medieval England: 1066 to the early fourteenth century with the main social, political and religious features of society. Evidence includes brasses, graves, documents.
Unit 10 Local study – settlement and change	History and geography. Changing patterns of settlement round a nearby city – in particular the Roman and medieval periods. Fieldwork.
Unit 11 (Geography)	Atlas, world features.
Unit 12 Maps and world topics	Europe discovers the world. The unit builds on skills developed in Unit 11.
Unit 13 (Geography)	Meteorology.
Unit 14 (Social science	Comparative study of primitive societies. Masai, Inuit (Eskimos), Aboriginals, village life in India. The emphasis is away from a Eurocentric syllabus.

Year 3

Unit 14, unit 16, unit 17 Social, economic, technological and social change	Swindon before and after the impact of the transport revolution. The growth of Swindon as a railway town. The growth of a modern town and inner urban problems: conflicts over the use of space, transport, pollution, neighbourhood and 'ghetto' problems.

Years 4 and 5

Either 2 O-levels or 2 CSEs or 1 of each

O-levels:
History and geography; Social sciences
CSEs:
Humanities; Social Studies

Overlapping syllabuses. All build in the first three years and seek to encourage skills as well as the acquisition of knowledge, eg selecting, asking analytical questions, forming hypotheses, analysing and evaluating data, and communicating. The emphasis is on relating the nature of the physical world to social and economic aspects of behaviour.

The course concentrates on six main themes:

- the family, its changing structure and function in modern times;
- Education. Changes in its structure and function. The impact of the media;
- work and leisure. The effects of automation; technological change. Changing patterns of work and leisure in industrial societies;
- urban and rural developments;
- population, poverty and development: in particular, world population changes, the distribution of wealth. Economic and political causes;
- war and peace in the twentieth century. Political and diplomatic developments since 1918.

History, geography, social sciences 8 to 13: Place, time and society[1]

In 1971, the Schools Council funded a major project to establish a rationale for the teaching of history, geography and the social sciences for children between the ages of 8 and 13. Working with teachers in primary, middle and secondary schools, the staff of the project established that the need was to support teachers' own thinking in exploring place, time and society rather than to produce yet another ready-made course in the humanities, complete with a kit of teaching materials. As a result, the project suggested ways to help teachers select, plan and organise the work in these areas of the curriculum.

These depend on two related strategies. The first helps teachers to distinguish objectives in history, geography and the social sciences in terms of intellectual, social and physical skills and pupil interest, attitudes and values. The second helps teachers to come to terms with these areas of the curriculum by using key concepts[2] common to the three disciplines.

The first group of concepts concerns elements that are present in all societies whatever their geographical or historical location: *communication, power, values and beliefs* and *conflict and consensus*. The other three concepts provide ways of analysing societies through their *similarities and differences* the *continuities and changes* that can be distinguised in them, and the *causes and consequences* of people's actions in relation to themselves, to others and to the environment. Although the key concepts and ideas are not designed to be taught directly to pupils, they can help teachers select themes and topics and design units of work which in turn will help gradually to build up in pupils' minds a picture of what they mean.

The project does not set out to promote the integration of history, geography and the social sciences, but rather to increase the opportunities for *planned* links between these subjects as an aid to learning and understanding. In offering teachers help in implementing these processes, the project developed a number of units of work, embodying the principles of the process, which act as exemplars for teachers in preparing their own, strategies.

The project also produced booklets on curriculum planning, games and simulations, evaluation and assessment, as well as on teaching for concepts, empathy and thinking skills. These booklets and the resource units offer practical guidance to the teacher. When the units were tried out in the project schools, ideas such as empathy, critical judgement, and the establishment of testing of hypotheses were explored, and these too have particular relevance for history. In sum, the project attempted to provide the means for teachers to select and organise subject matter on principles more consistent than habit, opportunism or personal inclination, though none of these would necessarily be excluded. It has been particularly influential in helping to order the thinking of many (especially local education authority advisers) concerned with humanities – and particularly history – in the middle years.

History 13–16

The Schools Council project *History 13 to 16*[3] which was first funded in 1972, has suggested ways in which a scheme of work can be structured so that it allows pupils to experience a variety of historical content and methods. It starts with the premise that pupils can begin to see that history is a subject that is useful to them, provided that the syllabus framework makes this clear, that teaching and learning involve the use of historical evidence and enquiry, and that teachers discuss the implications of all this with the pupils. Thus it suggests a syllabus framework for 14 to 16 year olds that includes studies in modern world history, a depth study involving fieldwork of the history around us in the environment. It also produces sample materials for some topics that become the basis for an *external* examination course at both GCE level and CSE.[4] It argues that such studies help to explain the present for pupils by giving them the widening experience of studying peoples of a different time and place. It provides materials for the understanding of change and causation in human affairs and contributes to leisure interests. It also suggests that this framework can be used as a basis for the syllabus in the earlier school years before the age of 14.

The Project also attempts to meet some of the needs of young people by helping them to understand their present world, people of a different time, and how change occurs in human affairs, and to develop leisure interests in the historical environment.

To meet these aims, the Project, in the first place, introduces young people to a unit called 'What is history?'. This was originally intended to be a one-term course for 13 year olds, but it – or strategies related to it – are now widely used throughout the 11 to 14 age range. It starts with the idea of the historian as a detective, and seeks to introduce pupils not only to the nature of history but to some of its basic skills, particularly those concerned with evidence. The work centres on a number of individual cases which raise problems and pose questions, such as the Sutton Hoo burial ship, Richard III and the missing princes, and the death of the suffragette Emily Davison at the 1913 Derby.

[1] *Place, Time and Society* materials are published by Collins.

[2] For an explanation of 'concept' see page 14.

[3] Further details of the project can be obtained from: Schools Council Project: History 13–16, Trinity and All Saints' Colleges, Brownberrie Lane, Horsforth, Leeds LS18 5HD.

[4] In particular, the examination syllabusés from: University of Cambridge Local Examination Syndicate, Syndicate Buildings, 17 Harvey Road, Cambridge CB1 2EU, and Southern Regional Examination Board, Avondale House, 33 Carlton Crescent, Southampton, Hampshire SO9 4YL.

'What is history?' is followed by a two-year course ending in an examination at GCE O-Level and at CSE. The syllabus consists of four main sections. First, there is a study in development, which emphasises the significance of change through time and other important ideas such as 'anachronism', 'continuity', and 'causation'. Its theme is the history of medicine from early man to the present. An additional option on 'Energy through Time' will be added shortly. Secondly, there is also an inquiry in depth into one short period. It seeks, for example, to examine the complicated relationship between people and events, and to understand the attitudes and values of people in other times. This inquiry has three options: Elizabethan England, Britain 1815–1851, and the American West 1840–1890. Thirdly, there are four studies in modern world history from which either one or two may be selected:

'The Rise of Communist China'
'The Move to European Unity'
'The Arab-Israeli Conflict'
and 'The Irish Question'.
'Japan – the silent superpower' will be a further option.
Lastly, there is 'History around us'.

This offers a series of possible themes, ranging from prehistoric Britain, through castles and the making of the rural landscapes, to industrial archaeology. This section is assessed as course work and involves young people in fieldwork, developing their powers of critical evaluation and their observation of visible evidence. The examination paper also contains an important section asking a series of questions of the use of evidence based on unseen material.

The strategy of the Project, particularly in its selective approach to content does not suit all teachers. Nevertheless, it is becoming one of the most popular of examination options. Its approach to the use of evidence is influencing the teaching of history in many of the schools that are teaching only part of the course – and, indeed, in many that are teaching none of it. Its importance lies in its attempt to identify and describe a series of progressively demanding stages within historical skills and the means of assessing them. These suggest important ways forward, not only towards assessment in examinations that may be based on grade descriptions but also towards the major effect assessment may have on teaching styles.

APPENDIX 2: FRAMEWORKS OF THE PAST

Framework 1

The Greeks	The Reformation	Growth of parliamentary democracy
The Roman Empire	The English Revolution of the 17th Century	From Empire to Commonwealth and multi-cultural Britain
The coming of Christianity		
The Norman Conquest	Industrial Revolution	The Russian Revolution
The spread of Islam	The American Revolution	Britain's Welfare State
The Renaissance	The French Revolution	World Wars One and Two

Framework 2

9000 – 8000 BC	Domestication of animals and crops 'Neolithic Revolution' (Middle East and North Africa)
	Hunters spread South through the Americas
c. 4000 BC	Bronze casting in Middle East
c. 2590 BC	Cheops builds great pyramid at Giza
c. 1600 BC	Shang Dynasty China 'Shang Bronze Age Culture'
c. 1500 BC	Ideographic script used in China, linear B in Crete etc
c. 1150 BC	King David unites Israel and Judah
486 BC	Death of Siddhartha Gautama, founder of Buddhism
480 BC	Battles of Salamis and Plataea, Persian invasion of Greece defeated
329 BC	Alexander the Great reaches the Oxus (India)
262 BC	Asoka, Mauryan emperor (273 BC – 236 BC) converted to Buddhism
49 BC	Julius Caesar conquers Gaul
c. 30 AD	Jesus of Nazareth crucified in Jerusalem
410 AD	Sack of Rome by Visigoths
486 AD	Frankish Kingdom founded by Clovis
c. 600 AD	Apogee of Mayan Civilisation
622 AD	Hegira of Mohammed: beginning of Islamic Calendar
624 AD	China united under Tang dynasty
700 AD	Rise of the kingdom of Ghana
732 AD	Battle of Poitiers

Framework 2 continued

800 AD	Charlemagne crowned Emperor: beginning of Holy Roman Empire
853 AD	First book printed in China
900 AD	Gunpowder in China
c. 900 AD	Expansion of Inca Empire
c. 1000 AD	First Iron Age settlement at Zimbabwe
1325 AD	Rise of Aztecs in Mexico
1445 AD	Johannes Gutenburg (1379 – 1468) prints first book in Europe
1453 AD	Ottoman Turks capture Constantinople
1478 AD	Ivan III, subdues Novgorod and throws off Mongol yoke
1492 AD	Columbus reaches Americas
1493 AD	Treaty of Tordesillas
1498 AD	Vasco da Gama reaches India via Cape of Good Hope
1452–1519 AD	Leonardo da Vinci
1519 AD	Magellan circumnavigates the world
1519 AD	Cortes conquest of Aztec Empire
1521 AD	Martin Luther outlawed
1526 AD	Battle of Panipat. Babur conquers the kingdom of Delhi and founds Mughal dynasty
1532 AD	Pizarro conquest of Inca Empire
1571 AD	Battle of Lepanto
1607 AD	First permanent English settlement in North America, Jamestown Virginia
1609 AD	Beginning of Tokugawa shogunate in Japan
1618 AD	Beginning of the Thirty Years War
1642 AD	English Civil War begins
1644 AD	Manchus found new dynasty (Ch'ing) in China
1645 AD	Tasman circumnavigates Australia and discovers New Zealand
1709 AD	Abraham Darby discovers coke smelting technique
1757 AD	Battle of Plassey: Clive establishes power in India
1775 AD	American Revolution begins
1789 AD	French Revolution begins
1818 AD	Shaka forms Zulu nation
1824 AD	Battle of Ayacucho – Bolivar and San Martin
1835 AD	Great Trek of Boer colonists from Cape leading to establishment of Orange Free State, Natal and Transvaal
1848 AD	Communist Manifesto issues by Marx and Engels
1856 AD	Bessemer process permits mass-production of steel
1857 AD	Indian Mutiny

continued overleaf

Framework 2 continued

1861 AD	Outbreak of the American Civil War
1869 AD	Suez Canal opens
1901 AD	Boxer rebellion
1911 AD	Chinese Revolution – Sun Yat-Sen First President
1917 AD	Russian Revolution
1920 AD	Mustafa Kemal (Ataturk) leads Turkish Nationalist Movement
1933 AD	Hitler made Chancellor in Germany
1941 AD	Fall of Singapore
1945 AD	Yalta Conference. Cold War begins
1945 AD	Atomic bomb used on Hiroshima and Nagasaki
1945 AD	Dien Bien Phu defeat of French in Indo China
1947 AD	Independence of India and Pakistan
1949 AD	Communist victory in China
1957 AD	Independence of Ghana
1962 AD	Cuban missile crisis
1967 AD	Third Arab-Israeli War (Six-Day War)
1971 AD	OPEC set up

Framework 3

Framework 3 is used in a comprehensive school in Wales. The head of the history department writes:

"We begin in our course at the school by presenting a brief outline of world history, organised under fifty headings and into groups whose initial letters form mnemonic words which can be easily learned by pupils:

ASCBITA
Ancestor of Man
Stone Ages
City Dwellers
Bronze and Iron Ages
Imperial Chinese Dynasties
Thinkers of the Ancient World
Alexander and Asoka

RODMAN
Romans
Our Lord
Dark Ages
Mohammedans
African Kingdoms
Norsemen

CAMMBORE
Crusaders
Americans before Columbus
Mongols
Medieval Europe
Black Death
Ottoman Turks
Renaissance
Explorers

RASTELP
Reformation
Akbar
Scientific Revolution
Tokugawa Shogunate
English Revolutions
Louis XIV of France
Peter the Great of Russia

SAFILEMMIS
Seven Years War
American War of Independence
French Revolution
Industrialisation
Latin American Independence
Evolution
Marx
Marconi
Imperialism
Sigmund Freud

HERTSAWMONOS
Heavier than Air Flight
Einstein
Russian Revolution
Treaty of Versailles
Stalin
Adolf Hitler

World War II
Mao Tse Tung
Olympics of 1972
Nixon
OPEC
Semi-Conductors

The list is learned by rote, and at the same time, the pupils are taught a small amount of information to go with each item. For example, the Black Death:

'Bubonic Plague, carried by rats, killed off one person in three in Medieval Europe, and also, in particular, destroyed the prosperity of Haverfordwest. Survivors sometimes did well out of the Black Death: being fewer in number, they were often able to get higher pay, etc.'.

We conclude by offering pupils a 500-word summary of the course, chronologically running together many of the topics covered.

Finally, our orthodox twentieth-century history course also enables valuable insights to be made that contribute to a better understanding of the society we live in. Most pupils study the two World Wars; a portion of this time is spent looking at people from the West Indies and Africa, in particular, those who gave their lives or time for the 'mother country'. This is an unfashionable view for some. It is also an historical reality. We are certainly trying to debunk old myths, but, we hope, not at the expense of creating new ones."

APPENDIX 3: HISTORY AND MATHEMATICS

Background

The HMI 'Red Book' on the curriculum (*Curriculum 11-16*) drew attention to certain areas of experience to which all pupils should be exposed by the time they are 16. Later, the book described how certain subjects, such as history, geography or mathematics, might help schools in their efforts to introduce young people to these areas of experience. Eight such areas were suggested: the aesthetic and creative, the ethical, the linguistic, the mathematical, the physical, the scientific, the social and political, and the spiritual. Subsequently in the Curriculum Matters booklet *The Curriculum from 5 to 16* 'technological' has been added as a ninth area. Clearly, mathematics would be the most effective means of introduction to the mathematical area, but other subjects also have important roles to play in this task. The 'Red Book' listed 20 mathematical objectives – areas of competence that should be enjoyed by the average 16 year old.

The majority of pupils aged 9 to 13 study history, and this paper concentrates on that age range; it also suggests, some possibilities for more advanced links between history and mathematics at 16-plus.

This paper confines itself to considering average pupils and normal courses of work. When ages are cited, they are approximate guides. Mathematics is a subject where differences in ability often appear early and become rapidly more marked; thus, although work might be pitched far higher for some 12 or 13 year olds than might be implied here, yet it would not be realistic to suggest such exacting aims for the majority of pupils.

The main way in which history and mathematics can be brought more closely together is by ensuring that historians and mathematicians know more about each others work. Many normal history syllabuses provide opportunities for mathematics and history to work together to the benefit of both subjects. Furthermore, ordinary history courses contain elements that need mathematical precision if they are to avoid loose or unhelpful descriptions of past events. How many ships were there in the Spanish armada? How wealthy was Lorenzo the Magnificent? How do we measure the poverty of a medieval serf? How large was the empire of Kublai Khan? Very often historians need definite answers to such questions rather than adjectives and general impressions.

Terms

One useful curricular strategy is to list the technical terms that ought to be understood by pupils at certain stages in their development. Some of these terms are suggested by other sections of this paper and they might include (by the age of 13):

add, subtract, multiply, divide;

probable, possible;

decade, century, generation, millennium, average, cycle;

percentage, proportion, ratio, scale;

early, middle, late;

units of measure.

Number work

In communicating with each other, we often use quantitative descriptions; this means of expression is, arguably, increasing in our day and ought to increase precision in communication for it helps us to harden statements and ideas which, as Dr Johnson noted, formerly 'floated in the mind indefinitely'.

The necessary foundation for any number in history is the ability to carry out practical activities involving the ideas of addition, subtraction, multiplication and division. By performing these and other suggested tasks in history (or any other subject where such operations fit into the task in hand without being too contrived), mathematics not only supports the subject, but also benefits itself by getting practical application 'across the curriculum'.

The most familiar number work to historians is simple *statistical analysis*. By 11-plus, young historians ought to be able to handle simple statistics relating to the period or place they are studying, and to compare them with some norm – contemporary Great Britain, for example. Such data might be: population numbers, birth and death rates, expectation of life, prices, and the speed of travel by various means. To perform these tasks a pupil will have to be able to recognise and interpret percentages, fractions and decimals as well as various kinds of large numbers that appear in history work: thousands, tens of thousands, millions and billions (and perhaps the useful milliard, familiar on mainland Europe although less so in Britain). Finally, because much of this kind of information is tabulated, pupils should be able to both read and construct comparative tables of statistics. Thus, a young historian ought to be able to:

- collect statistics
- record, organise, interpret and present data
- make reasonable extrapolations from given data
- visualise accurately numbers of people; relative size and extent.

Ordering the data

Another important task for young historians is the ordering of data in sequence, placing historical events in correct series. At its simplest, this means that pupils should be familiar with the time chart so that they put, for example, the dinosaurs, the crusades and Queen Victoria in the correct order. Given the recent fashion for topic work, this is crucial for history and humanities courses in the middle years. If it is ignored, all kinds of anachronisms and scale distortions can result. At a more sophisticated level, say 13 to 16, placing events in correct historical sequence is a necessary part of any investigation that looks at cause and effect or at change in history. It may be that history work can give useful practice in other forms of ordering (eg alphabetical or by magnitude); nevertheless, chronological ordering is the most common and useful form employed by historians.

With an increased range of reference, a pupil ought also to be able to look at historical data and see if they are realistic – that is, to make sensible *estimates*, to distinguish between possiblity and probability. Estimates could relate to some of the data given

above in the section on statistical analysis: population and group sizes, territorial extent, and prices. Work of this kind will be valuable practice, relating mathematics to problems of the real world in the manner advocated by the Cockroft report, *Mathematics Counts* (1982).[1]

24 Christ and Dividers

Measures in history

So far, this paper has looked at the possibilities inherent in young historians' handling of simple data, numbers and straightforward mathematical ideas. However, a great deal of history work will deal inevitably with *units of measurement*, and as children get older (12-plus) they are more likely to come across obsolete units, or units that require further description and processing before they can be understood clearly.

For the most part, pupils ought to employ units of measure now in force: SI units and, where still applicable, imperial units.

The study of history will still require knowledge of obsolete units, and pupils should be able to convert these into contemporary units. Where monetary units are being dealt with, it is

important that pupils have a clear idea of the value of money during the past era under study. Textbooks are not always helpful on this matter, and original sources, such as historical documents, cannot, naturally, be expected to give any guidance. Therefore, pupils should know where to go for help, eg good dictionaries, encyclopaedias and other sources.

The most common problems (as missed opportunities) are:

- failure to convert old sterling to current prices; thus we hear that a Tudor house 'cost £60' or (from a textbook): 'The Asiento . . . was surrendered in 1750 in return for a payment from Spain of £1000,000'. If values of these figures are not appreciated then they are quite misleading, even meaningless. If they are appreciated, then they provide a most valuable example of *change through time*, one of the main ideas imparted by the study of history. Also, some useful economic understanding can come through such work. There are various sources of currency conversion such as the comparative tables produced by certain clearing banks;

- failure to convert exotic units of measurement into present-day values or otherwise to define or explain them, eg 100,000 'silver marks', £5 Scots; or to define obsolete units: groat, farthing, piece-of-eight, pagoda. The same consideration applies to units measuring length, area or volume: versts, quintals, li, cadastrals, and so on. This problem is confined more to 14-plus and, more particularly, to 16-plus work. It is as important for history pupils to be prepared for this difficulty as it is necessary for authors and publishers to be helpful on the matter.

Time

Clearly, an understanding of time, and familiarity with the measurement of its

[1]*Mathematics counts*. Report of the Committee of Inquiry into the teaching of Mathematics in Schools under the Chairmanship of Dr W H Cockcroft. HMSO, 1982.

passage, are essential skills for historians. A great deal of pedagogical writing has been devoted to the problem of children's understanding of time.

Teachers should ensure:

that children are conversant with the technical terms by which we measure the passage of time: centuries, decades, AD, BC, and so on. They should also be competent in handling the calendar and in understanding its working and terminology.

that children can calculate spans of time, eg how many years elapsed between 1378 and 1445, or between 35BC and AD77.

that children are given encouragement to appreciate and visualise passages of time, to acquire a time-sense. Although expert opinion differs on this question, there is no doubt that from the age of 9 onwards some children display the ability to talk in more refined terms about relative duration. Time charts will help them to put events in correct sequence. Other graphic means can help them to understand time-perspective, eg clock-faces that relate to the history of our planet, confining recorded human history to the last few seconds, or symbolic calendars that confine human history to a few minutes at the end of December. Given the opportunity, it is encouraging to see how many children aged 9 and over will rise to the occasion and find interest and illumination in such descrptions. These approaches also introduce children to the common social usages and assumptions regarding the passage of time.

Thus by 14 a pupil ought to be able to:

appreciate and describe relative tracts of time; have developed a frame of reference into which historical phenomena can be placed in correct order.

Without such a framework, peculiar anachronisms can develop, and so it is necessary to have a formally planned approach to the skill of placing events *in series* correctly.

Space

Curriculum 11-16 thought that 16 year olds ought to be able to 'handle . . . discuss, write about three-dimensional objects . . . solve problems about them by . . . scale drawings, interpretation of diagrams, plans and maps'. The drawing and interpreting of maps comes early in history and is not uncommon before 11. Other forms of spatial work found in history are model-making and drawing artefacts of the past. Such work ought to be done in such a way as to develop precision in the use of scales; a common fault is to allow cramped pictures and unscaled maps to appear in exercise books or folders. This is a good example of the way in which already familiar work can be made much more effective by relating it to some definite curricular plan. Maps, models and diagrams are already very common in 9 to 13 history work, but they are too rarely part of a cross-curricular strategy of developing skills. Thus it is a question of doing the same syllabus more effectively rather than scrapping familiar approaches and taking on new and relatively untried ones.

Communication

Although straightforward numbers will be the most usual form of mathematical communication in history, yet there are other and important means by which mathematical ideas can be conveyed. For example, a course of history for pupils aged 9 to 13, and certainly 14 to 16, gives ample scope for:

● pie charts eg proportions of the population in feudal times who were nobility, churchman, peasantry, etc);

● bar charts and histograms eg numbers of people dying before maturity from the Middle Ages up to modern times);

● graphs (eg rise in the price of bread or fall in the price of electric light);

● special forms of maps and diagrams which emphasise, for example, relative journey times rather than distances;

● three-dimensional models and maps.

An additional advantage of these and other varieties of graphic communication is, of course, that a picture 'is worth a thousand words', and is often more precise. Familiarity with these forms of 'graphicacy' is becoming an essential part of the intellectual equipment of educated people in technological societies, and history is an effective way in which to introduce this mathematical usage into the study of society.

History of mathematics

This term may sound formidable if one is considering the education of pupils aged 9 to 16. However, the history of mathematics has two aspects from the standpoint of this publication. First, there are simple facts and ideas about the mathematical attainments and achievements of our ancestors that give straightforward and yet dramatic insights into the nature of past societies and illuminate the ideas of contrast and change. Secondly, there is a more specialist and academic aspect to the problem that may be of restricted although important use to the 16 to 19 phase of education.

One of the enduring debates in history is over the nature of 'progress' – is humanity better or better off now than formerly? How do we measure or perceive change? Young people usually enjoy this debate and are quite capable of making sensible contributions to it, given data and guidance. The mathematical considerations of this problem are many. The mathematical considerations of this problem are many. A few of them are:

● that although our understanding of mathematics has clearly progressed and become more refined, yet many past societies had mathematical systems of great refinement themselves. This consideration may help to mitigate the coarser and less critical notions lying behind the notion of progress. For example, the achievement of the Greek, Eratosthenes, in measuring the size of the Earth (240 BC), the existence of the highly accurate and advanced calendar of the ancient Mayan civilization, or the geometry and astronomy of our megalithic ancestors – all these are examples of powerful mathematical thinking;

• the necessity for accurate measurement that lies behind a great deal of fundamental technology. History courses already abound with outward and visible signs of this fact, although they may not draw sufficient attention to it. The manufacture of weapons, the building of castles and pyramids, the navigation of the oceans – all of these important achievements depended upon forms of mathematical skill;

• different societies have measured and recorded in different ways. By 14, a pupil ought to know and to be able to use Roman as well as Arabic numerals; to realise that the Jewish or Islamic calendars use different starting points, and why this is so. To understand this feature of civilisation is to begin to see unity in diversity – different outward forms, but similar underlying principles. Thus, the oriental abacus, the knotted string of the Incas or the pocket calculator of today may be seen as contrasting methods of accomplishing common tasks: coding, recording and computing;

• nevertheless, the development of mathematical techniques suggests gradual yet perceptible development of two features: greater refinement through time, and increasing employment of a common language shared and enjoyed by people all over

the world. While a normal course of history can draw attention to these features, it is also crucial that history work makes it clear that 'progress' is by no means always so clear to beneficial as this story might imply.

Older and more advanced pupils may well benefit from more difficult work in the history of mathematics. This could be a feature of either advanced history or mathematics courses, or of general studies work in the 16 to 19 area. 'History' in this age range is often political, although economic and social history have gained ground in recent years. Teachers can best gauge how much mathematical history, and how advanced, is appropriate for their pupils. Non-mathematicians ought to be aware, at the very least, of some important mathematicians whose work has made other forms of intellectual and practical achievement possible. For example a student of the seventeenth century who was completely ignorant of Kepler, Newton or Leibnitz would be a very partial historian indeed. However, a student would need to have considerable mathematical skill to have real insight into the work of these men, or of later mathematicians like Euler, Gauss or Cauchy. The same could be said concerning really detailed study of the work of the ancients alluded to above – Euclidean geometry or Ptolemaic astronomy, for example. There is also the long and venerable history of pre-seventeenth century Chinese mathematics with its strong algebraic tradition of using words as symbols; which is, regrettably, for that reason largely unknown in the West. It

is as important for young mathematicians as it is for young historians to realise that mathematics, like architecture, music and technology, is more definitely *not* a post-Renaissance western invention.

Conclusion

A few modest strategies are suggested in this Appendix by which orthodox history courses can help in the task of developing mathematical understanding and skills. To do so in no way distorts or diminishes history work – far from it, such an approach improves history by making it more precise in its handling of data and in its attempts to communicate the results of its debates. Although history is largely a literary activity, there is no logical reason why it should be exclusively so; indeed, it has a long tradition of employing mathematical techniques in certain areas – in economic and social history, for example, where mathematics has given form and precision to the study of trade, industry, populations, and the creation and distribution of wealth.

This Appendix is in no way suggesting 'integrated studies' between history and mathematics; but it does advocate most strongly that these two important subjects should reinforce each other, and that all schools ought to have a clear and agreed strategy by which this work can be done.

Printed for Her Majesty's Stationery Office by Linneys Colour Print
Dd 738301 C125 9/85 43732